I0112012

THE
CHRISTIAN COUNSELOR'S
COMMENTARY

ACTS

JAY E. ADAMS

MID-AMERICA
INSTITUTE FOR NOUTHETIC STUDIES

Institute for Nouthetic Studies, a ministry of Mid-America Baptist
Theological Seminary, 5640 Airline Road, Arlington, TN 38002
mabts.edu / nouthetic.org / INSBookstore.com

Acts: The Christian Counselor's Commentary
by Jay E. Adams
Copyright © 2025 by the Institute for Nouthetic Studies,
© 1994 by Jay E. Adams

ISBN: 978-1-970445-01-5 (Paper)
ISBN: 978-1-970445-02-2 (eBook)
Old ISBN: 0-889032-09-3

Editor: Donn R. Arms

Library of Congress Cataloging-in-Publication Data
Names: Adams, Jay E., 1929-2020
Title: *I & II Timothy, Titus:*
The Christian Counselor's Commentary
by Jay E. Adams
Description: Arlington, TN: Institute for Nouthetic Studies, 2025
Identifiers: ISBN 978-1-970445-01-5 (paper) | OCLC: 33193289
Classification: LCC BS2745.3 .A434 | DDC 227.87

All rights reserved. No part of this publication may be reproduced, stored
in a retrieval system, or transmitted in any form or by any means –
electronic, mechanical, photocopy, recording, or any other – except for
brief quotations in printed reviews, without prior permission of the
publisher.

Published in the United States of America

Introduction

When I began the New Testament Commentary series several years ago, the first volume covered the two letters of Paul to the Corinthians.[1] At that time I had nothing more than an overall plan for covering the corpus of New Testament books. I did not know which would be the last volume or the order in which I would be able to publish the series. As it so happens, through much deliberation along the way, and after an excursion into publishing one Old Testament book in the series (Proverbs[2]), I now am undertaking the task of commentating on the book of Acts, thus completing the entire series.

At a juncture such as this, it is probably well to pause for a moment to speak about the project that is now drawing to a close. When I translated the *Christian Counselor's New Testament*, I noted in the introduction how much personal value I had received from the effort. I would not have missed that opportunity for anything. The same conviction now grips me as I launch out to work on the last volume of the commentary series. I have personally profited from this endeavor more than in any other effort that I have ever expended. I cannot recommend too highly to anyone and everyone who can do so to follow a similar course. There is no other way to become as fully acquainted with the Lord's Word as for one to interpret and comment about it himself. I have tried to be faithful, but I am sure that there are matters that could be improved. Yet, for whatever value it may have, I send it forth with the hope that it will benefit many.[3]

The Book of Acts

The book of Acts is not a record of the Acts of the Apostles, as it has been wrongly titled.[4] Rather, as we shall see, it contains acts of only three apostles (Peter, John,[5] Paul). It was never intended to be an account of the

---

[1] Reasons for this are given in the introduction to that volume.

[2] This was not originally planned, but became necessary to counseling.

[3] I have received encouraging evaluations of the commentaries as they have been successively appearing that not only have given me some assurance that they have been well received by many, but also that they have been hoping for the completion of the entire series.

[4] The original manuscript had no title. The uninspired title was added years later.

[5] And John, only to a minor extent.

apostles' works after the ascension of the Lord Jesus Christ. The book concerns not the acts of apostles—even the two prominent ones[1]—but rather gives an account of how the church spread from Jerusalem to Rome.[2]

The title, Acts (as I shall continue to call it), is not altogether inappropriate, however. I say that because it is a book about the acts of Jesus Christ through the Holy Spirit, Whom He sent from the heavens to take His place among the disciples and the members of the church. In the first verse of the Acts, Luke tells us his gospel concerns all that Jesus **began** both to do and to teach until the day when He was taken up to heaven. The emphasis in the original language is on the word **began**, signaling to us that after His ascension He *continues* to act and teach, now through the Spirit, and that in this second volume Luke says that he will delineate these things. The book of Acts is filled with references to the Holy Spirit, so much so that it might be appropriately titled, The Acts of the Holy Spirit. There are about 70 references to the Holy Spirit in Acts alone, one-fifth of the references in the entire New Testament. *He* is the principal Actor, not the apostles.

As Jesus had outlined (Acts 1:8), the Spirit would come and see that the message was powerfully preached in Jerusalem, then in Judea and Samaria and, finally, to the ends of the earth (represented by Rome—the capital of the civilized world). But just how was this missionary enterprise carried out? Acts describes it in detail.

Once, a missionary studying in one of my graduate classes in preaching made this statement: "In seminary I was trained to be a missionary, so I was given no training in preaching." Think of that! How times have changed. Missions, according to Acts, was a *preaching* enterprise. Stand back and take a panoramic look at the book as a whole. It is a series of messages—sermons and speeches—strung along a narrative about the church's spreading from Jerusalem to Rome by the preaching of the gospel to all sorts and conditions of men.[3] If Acts demonstrates anything, it is

---

[1] The book is largely the story of an apostle who was not one of the original twelve.

[2] Luke is not primarily interested in the men God used to spread the church; his concern is strictly for them as "witnesses" whom the Spirit used to do so. There are seven reports concerning the progress of the church. These occur at 2:47, 6:7, 9:31, 12:24, 16:5, 19:20, and 28:31. The idea of reporting the growth of the church demonstrates this concern of the author.

[3] Three hundred out of the one thousand verses in Acts are devoted to sermons

that the Holy Spirit's mission was principally carried on by preaching. There is no way to conclude anything else by studying the book itself. Indeed, before He left them, Jesus told His disciples that the Holy Spirit would prepare and guide them in all their preaching in a unique way.[1]

Preaching was extremely important to the work of missions. And so was counseling, as we shall see in the discussion of Acts 20. Counseling followed the preaching as the means of establishing the infant congregations in their newly-found faith. Because preaching and counseling are but two sides of the same ministry of the same Word to the same people to meet the same problems and needs, there is also much for counselors to learn from this inspired preaching. The crossover from the one to the other is not very great. Acts, therefore, will be a valuable book for our study from many angles and will, in a number of ways, provide a climax to the whole series of New Testament commentaries.

Furthermore, many commentators have spoken about the seeming incompleteness of Acts. There are reasons for this. First, as I have noted, it is not the story of Peter or Paul. Peter disappears from its pages after chapter 15, just as Paul does after chapter 28. Though we would like to know what happened to both, it is not Luke's (or the Holy Spirit's) purpose to tell us. He is primarily interested in the message and the mission—and only in the men in a secondary sense. Consider also the fact that the book was written to the "most excellent" Theophilus (cf. Luke 1:1-4; Acts 1:1, 2). The term *kratistos* ("most excellent") means that Theophilus held some sort of office in the Roman government.[2] It is possible that he had become a Christian and was now interceding for Paul in his imprisonment. Acts could have been a sort of brief that Luke prepared for him. But it must also be recognized that the book of Acts was just about the length of a complete papyrus roll (30 feet long). There could have been little more included than there was. And, finally, all discussions must come down to this: the book of Acts was complete for its purposes.

In this book we shall at times focus more intensively on a section here and there as it particularly provides extensive material for counselors. In other places we shall move more quickly, especially in the last few chapters, as the narrative swiftly carries us forward. All in all, I trust that you will find Acts most valuable to you as a biblical counselor.

---

and speeches.

[1] We'll take a look at this in our discussion of chapter two.

[2] Luke uses the term in Acts 23:26, 24:2, and 26:25 to indicate respect for office.

CHAPTER 1

1 In the former account, Theophilus, I wrote about all that Jesus began to do and teach

2   until the day that He was taken up, after He had given instructions to the apostles whom He had chosen through the Holy Spirit.

As we begin to consider the book of Acts in relationship to biblical counseling, we shall find that the Holy Spirit[1] reveals much that is of value to the counselor. Some information will be directly related to counseling; most will be of an inferential nature that nevertheless is of great help.

The book opens with a reference to Luke's **former account** (the Gospel of Luke). Both Luke and Acts were written to the same man, Theophilus, a state official.[2] As Luke implies by placing the emphasis on the word **began**, the Gospel was only the beginning of what Jesus would **do and teach**. In Acts, he would continue to record the Acts of Jesus from heaven into which He **was taken up.** The apostles were chosen **through the Holy Spirit** Whom He soon would send to them. It is this Spirit, taking His place as the other Counselor (like Jesus[3]), Who would now instruct the **apostles whom He had chosen** (v. 2). In one sense we may say that the entire book of Acts is counsel from Jesus to His church through the Spirit. It is therefore significant to note those things that the Spirit directs His servants after Him, to **do and to teach.** We may fruitfully apply them to our counseling ministries as well as to preaching.

Notice that it is the Lord Who **chooses**, and is entirely in control of, those who will minister in His church (v. 2). There are too many today who, apart from any recognition from or ordination by the church, seek to lead—especially in writing and speaking about counseling, as well as in practicing counseling as a life calling. It is largely from them that erroneous and unbiblical views and practices in counseling stem. The Christian in the pew has not been sufficiently informed that he has been sold a bill of goods in this respect. Licensure from the state to counsel and ordination by the church to do so are two different things that lead to two differ-

---

[1] See comments in the Introduction concerning the place of the Spirit in Acts.

[2] See the Introduction for information on the words **most excellent**.

[3] Cf. John 14:16, 17. The word "another" means "another of the same kind."

> 3   It was to them also that, after He suffered, He presented Himself alive by many decisive proofs, appearing to them over a period of forty days and speaking about matters pertaining to God's empire.

---

ent outcomes. Passing a course of studies in psychiatry or psychology, with the attendant degrees, does not qualify one to counsel God's people about God's will for their lives. God chooses His leadership in the church which, according to the book of Acts as we shall see, confirms it by ordination.[1] Jesus Christ is the King and Head over His church, a kingship that He exercises from heaven through His Spirit Who works in and through the church.

The Lord Jesus affirmed His victory over Satan, sin and death by His resurrection from the dead and His appearance to His disciples **over a period of forty days** prior to His ascension (v. 3). During that time He was not idle. Indeed, He spent it **speaking about matters pertaining to God's empire**. Much of what we have been studying in the gospels and in the epistles—as well as what we shall learn from the book of Acts—was delivered by Jesus to them at the time. Doubtless many of their misunderstandings were cleared up; and much of their subsequent teaching and the enthusiasm and assurance needed to accomplish the tasks ahead was imparted to them. But not everything was understood or made clear at that time (as study of Acts will disclose). Jesus provided all that they needed immediately and all they could ingest. Throughout their ministries, they would learn more and more of what Jesus would continue to **do and to teach**.

Eating with them and encouraging the disciples to thrust their hands into His side were just two of the **decisive proofs** that Jesus gave them of His resurrection from the dead. We do not know what they all were, but there were **many**. No doubt, during this long transitional period that they spent with the risen Lord, the apostles not only learned much, but were also solidly grounded in the faith. They would need this grounding to face the innumerable obstacles that the evil one would place in their paths. They would need the certain assurance that Jesus was alive, and that they were sent by Him on their mission, to faithfully endure the excruciating persecutions and hardships that lay ahead. Jesus knew this and planned to spend this forty day period with them for these and other purposes He had in mind.

---

[1] Ordination means "setting aside" to a work.

4   During a meal with them He ordered them not to leave Jerusalem, but
to "wait for the fulfillment of the Father's promise that you heard about
from Me.
5   John baptized with water, but you will be baptized with the Holy Spirit
in a few days."
  6 So then, when they came together they asked Him, "Lord, is it at this
time that You will restore the kingdom to Israel?"

The Lord's consideration for His disciples and the depth of preparation He provided them should tell us something about the importance of
such things for those who are about to counsel others. Ministers of the
gospel are often thrown into the fray without adequate preparation and
without the necessary encouragement which comes from association with
their predecessors. If we are ever to spread the work of counseling in a
way that will tear down barriers and move it from Jerusalem to Rome, we
must spend more quality time with the generation of ministers to come.
The **instructions**[1] Jesus gave were in the form of a general's marching
orders. Some such set of biblical injunctions needs to be formulated for
those who would take up the counseling work that many of us are about to
lay down. Much more encouragement and practical instruction must
accompany it. And there must be more places where those who are about
to undertake the task can receive biblical answers to their questions.
     One of the proofs that Jesus had risen in a physical body was His eat-
ing of food. During one **meal** with His disciples, Luke tells us He gave
orders to **wait** for God to fulfill His promise of the coming Holy Spirit
(v. 4). Evidently, they were to make no moves and take no action until He
was present in His task as the One Who would empower and guide them
in their work. That promise, which they had heard previously, was
repeated: in contrast to John's baptism, in **a few days** they would be **baptized with the Holy Spirit** (v. 5). This, of course, was a prediction of the
Pentecostal event that is recorded in the next chapter. They failed to heed
this injunction, which we will see later in the present chapter.
     This brief period of a few days was a time in which the ignorance of
the apostles who did not yet have the Spirit was still evident. They were
looking for the fulfillment of the Judaistic hope of a kingdom **restored to
Israel**. They wanted to know if it would happen at that time. They still
didn't understand that He would ascend to be given the worldwide empire

---

[1] Literally, "orders, commands."

7   He said to them,
>   it is not for you to know the times or seasons that the Father has set by His own authority;

8   >   instead, you will receive power when the Holy Spirit has come upon you, and you will be My witnesses in Jerusalem, in the rest of Judea and Samaria, and to the ends of the earth.

9   When He had said this, He was taken up as they watched; a cloud took Him up from their sight.

---

promised in Daniel 2 and 7. They expected an earthly kingdom with Israel in ascendancy. Instead of answering the question in the form in which it had been posed, Jesus said that the **times and seasons** for things that God has **set** were not to be given to them. They were to follow instructions and not try to figure out matters about which they could not know until they occurred. He said nothing about the fact that they were wrong in their supposition that the kingdom would be restored to Israel, because in a few moments they would be witnesses of His ascension; and when the Holy Spirit came they would be able to comprehend and correctly preach the facts about which they were wondering.[1]

The important thing was not the answer to their question, Jesus intimates, but the fact that the **Holy Spirit** would come to give them **power** to spread the church throughout the *oikoumene* (the civilized world). As they preached, under His inspiration, they would learn as well as their hearers. All depended on His coming; they were to anticipate *that*.

The same is true today. Counselors may have many questions but they are to look for the guidance of the Spirit in His Word (the only place it may now be found), focusing on it alone in their counsel.[2] Many want what the Spirit hasn't given; but they will never counsel properly until they commit to the Scriptures alone. God's ministers are always faced with this contrasting choice—will they ignorantly seek irrelevant information or will they confine themselves to what God gives them?

The ascension immediately answered their question about the kingdom: Jesus would not remain on the earth to head up an earthly kingdom for Israel (vv. 9, 10). He was going to the Father, as they later understood and preached, to rule with all authority over heaven and earth.[3] He had

---

[1] Cf. Acts 2:22, 23, 36.

[2] For further help, see my book *The Christian's Guide to Guidance*.

[3] Cf. Matthew 28:18-20.

10 As they were gazing at the sky while He went, two men in white clothes stood by them

11 and said,

> Men of Galilee, why do you stand looking at the sky? This Jesus Who has been taken up from you into the sky will come back in the same way that you saw Him go into the sky.

12 Then they returned to Jerusalem from the Mount of Olives, which is close to Jerusalem, just a Sabbath's journey away.

13 When they arrived, they went up to the upper room where they were staying. There were Peter, John, James, Andrew, Philip, Thomas, Bartholomew, Matthew, James (Alphaeus' son), Simon (the Zealot) and Judas (James' son).

14 They were all with one mind, persevering in prayer together with the women and Mary, Jesus' mother, and His brothers.

15 Now in those days Peter stood up in the midst of the brothers (who on that occasion numbered about one hundred twenty) and said,

---

become (as the God-man) both Lord and Christ (Acts 2:36).

Two angels then appeared, explaining that the ascension would someday be followed by a return of the Savior in a similar manner (that is a visible, bodily return from the **sky**). That return we all still await (the angel did not say that the disciples would see it in their lifetime). Notice, again, the angel gave them just enough information to help them in the situation, not a full explanation. God often does the same in the Bible.

The apostles then returned to the little company in Jerusalem where in **prayer** and discussion they gathered to await the coming of the Spirit. (vv. 12-14). It is interesting that through their activities they came to be of **one mind**. There possibly had been a time when they were not. It is encouraging to see that Jesus' brothers did come to faith in Him (v. 14).[1]

Peter was still the impetuous spokesman for the gathering. He stood up and addressed the rest (v. 15). His address follows in verses 15 through 20. Peter, recognizing that the company of the twelve had been depleted because of the betrayal and subsequent death of Judas, suggested that they elect a successor. He explained that Judas' defection necessitated the a replacement and gave Old Testament proof texts to support his position. But was he right in doing so? Were the 120 disciples correct in moving ahead when Jesus had told them to **wait** for the Spirit? The calling of the apostle Paul as the replacement for Judas seems to have been the way in

---

[1] But where is Joseph?

5

16   Brothers, the Scripture that the Holy Spirit spoke beforehand through David's mouth about Judas, who became the guide of those who arrested Jesus, had to be fulfilled.

17   He was numbered among us and was allotted his share of this ministry.

18   (He then bought a field from the payment of his unrighteousness, and falling headlong his abdomen burst open and his intestines gushed out.

19   Everybody in Jerusalem learned about this, so that they called that field—in their own language—Akeldama, that is, "field of blood.")

20   It is written in the book of Psalms,
      Let his homestead be deserted;
      may nobody live in it; and,
      Let a different person take his office of oversight.

---

which God filled the vacancy. *He* was the One to choose His apostles, as we saw above. The 120 were about to receive supernatural help from the Spirit; yet, they were moving out on their own to make this crucial decision without His guidance.[1] They didn't **wait**. Peter was right about the prophecies to which he referred, but he was wrong about the way in which they would be fulfilled and about the person whom God would appoint. We hear nothing more of Matthias. Jesus would *personally* call Paul to the apostleship; there would be no *providential* calling through the use of **lots** (vv. 21-26).

The death of **Judas** is important. It shows how a person who is overwhelmed with guilt and grief can be so hardened and self-centered as to hang himself rather than repent of his sin. And look at the slimy trail he left behind (vv. 18, 19). People today try to justify suicide. "The person was driven to it," they say. "He couldn't help it," they think. But the Bible is clear about this. Suicide is the coward's way out. It is the way of one who will not face the consequences of his actions. It is the way of the person who thinks that there is nothing to face after death, or, if there is, God will be lenient with him regardless of his irresponsible behavior. It is the way of the person who cares more about himself than about those he leaves behind: "Let them grieve. Let them wonder, so long as I get myself out of this mess." It is a supremely self-centered act.

---

[1] There will not be 13 names of the apostles instead of 12 as John tells us (Revelation 21:14)!

6

21   Therefore, one of the men who has accompanied us during the whole time that Jesus went in and out among us

22   (beginning from John's baptism until the day when He was taken up from us) must become a witness to His resurrection along with us.

23 So they nominated two: Joseph, called Barsabbas, who was also called Justus, and Matthias.

24 Then they prayed, saying,

      Lord, Heart-knower of all men, show which one of these two You have chosen

25   to take the place in this ministry and apostleship from which Judas fell away to go to his own place.

26 Then they cast lots about them, and the lot fell on Matthias. So he was counted along with the eleven apostles.

In verse 21 Peter sets up the qualifications for the replacement: He must be **one who has accompanied us during the whole time that Jesus went in and out among us**. Yes, those were the *ordinary* qualifications for an apostle. Peter was wrong. God was to raise up an apostle in an *extraordinary* way, an apostle who, in other ways, would become the most extraordinary apostle of the twelve—the apostle Paul. Peter, apart from the work of the guiding Spirit, could not imagine such a thing. And, therein, he and the rest who went along—**all of one mind**—were wrong.[1] The Spirit had not yet come in power to Christ's church, so the church was without supernatural guidance during this brief interim. Counselors must never act on their own. They have the supernaturally given Scriptures that set forth all they need to know to conduct the affairs of the church, including its counseling ministry. What mistakes we make when we look elsewhere for guidance!

---

[1] Consensus doesn't mean correctness.

CHAPTER 2

1 When the day of Pentecost had arrived, they were all together in one place.

2 Suddenly, there came a sound from the sky like the rush of a violent wind, and it filled the whole house in which they were sitting.

3 There appeared to them what looked like split tongues of fire that sat on each one of them.

4 And they were all filled with the Holy Spirit and began to speak revelatory words in different languages as the Spirit gave them ability.

In chapter two Luke has recorded the fulfillment of the promise of Jesus Christ given in the previous chapter: the descent of the Holy Spirit of power. This event took place on **the day of Pentecost**, when the small group of 120 were **all gathered together in one place** (v. 1). The way in which Luke sets forth what *they* did when they were gathered together (chapter 1) seems to contrast with what *God* did at a later gathering of the infant church (chapter 2). Jesus had told them to **wait** for this event.

Suddenly (there was no warning; God seems to delight in surprising us), a sound came from the sky like the **rush of a violent wind** that filled the entire house. This house-filling sound must have been nearly deafening since it was loud enough to be heard also by many outside who came running to see what was happening (v. 6). In this way God Himself gathered these persons together to hear the first Christian sermon. Peter (along with the rest) took advantage of this miracle and preached the gospel to the crowd.

Three things occurred within the house at the coming of the sound: (1) there appeared something that looked like inverted, **split tongues of fire** that **sat upon each one of them**; (2) **they were all filled with the Holy Spirit and** (3) they **began to speak in different languages as the Spirit gave them ability**. There are important points to be made about each of these occurrences.

The tongues of fire that came down upon each head were a visible representation of the invisible descent of the Spirit. The fact that He had actually been given to them and that the promise was fulfilled was assured by this occurrence. The ability to speak in tongues was *not* the sign of the coming of the Spirit. The **tongues of fire** were the sign of the **power** with which they were being endued by the Spirit's descent. This was the reception of the power mentioned in 1:8. The filling of the Spirit was universal; **all 120 received** it. This filling, symbolized by the fire, happened to

5 Now there were devout Jews from every nation under the sky living at Jerusalem.

6   When this sound was heard, a crowd gathered. But they were confused, because each one heard them speaking in his own speech.

7   They were astounded and amazed, saying,

Look! Aren't all of these who are speaking Galileans?

8   So how is it that we hear, each in his own native speech—

9   Parthians, Medes, Elamites, those who live in Mesopotamia, Pontus and Asia,

10   Phrygia, Pamphylia, Egypt and the parts of Libya that belong to Cyrene and the visitors from Rome, both Jews and proselytes,

11   Cretans and Arabians—we hear them speaking in our languages the great acts of God?

12   They were all astounded and upset, saying to one another, "What does this mean?"

---

enable them to **speak in different languages**. The tongues speaking was therefore not a *sign* of the reception and the filling, but was an *outcome*, a result of it. The **ability** made it possible for the 120 to speak in the native languages[1] of all sorts of foreigners who had gathered together at Jerusalem for Pentecost. Charismatics who misunderstand the purpose of the ability to speak in foreign languages without having ever learned them usually say that the ability is a *sign* of the filling. That is not true. The ability was given for the practical purpose of using that ability, as the disciples did (vv. 5-11). Counselors will run up against this sort of misunderstanding from time to time and ought to be ready to set to rest the minds of those who have been troubled by it. Simply understanding these basic facts will go a long way toward dealing with many false and disturbing claims. Be clear about them yourself, and pass them on to counselees whenever necessary.

The people who heard the sound, and then heard the 120 speaking in languages they could not have known, **were astounded and amazed** (vv. 7, 12). They could not explain the phenomenon. Some, however, **mocked** and claimed they were drunk (as if that could account for what was happening!). But the majority, it seems, asked a very important question, **"What does this mean?"** (v. 12). In other words, they were asking for more information: "Tell me more about it." That is where you want your listener in preaching or in counseling to begin—with a desire to learn more. Those who come

---

[1] Three times Luke makes the point that these were true languages (cf. vv. 6, 8, 11).

13   Others, mocking, said, "They're filled with new wine!"

14 But Peter stood up with the eleven and lifted up his voice and with these revelatory words spoke to them:
> Men of Judea, and all those who live in Jerusalem, listen to what I say, and I will explain this to you.

---

with their minds made up (to explain away the teachings of the Scriptures that relate to their lives) will always find an excuse for not listening (i.e. **"they're filled with new wine"**). But the sincere listener can be known by his yearning to hear more of what you have to say. He is the one who is likely to end up saying, **what should we do?** (v. 37). And that is precisely the kind of movement that you want to see. You want the counselee to ask for more information, and then, having heard it, to say, "Where do I go from here?" That is the process of change that needs to take place in hearers of sermons or of instruction given in counseling. When you see that sort of movement in a counselee, you can be nearly certain that he is heading in the right direction.

Now, in verses 14 and following, we turn to Peter's sermon. He began not, as the seminary professors suggest, by winning approval from his audience, but by contradicting them (vv. 14, 15)! That is no way to win sermon prizes, you can be sure. Peter was motivated not by the approval of men, but by the Spirit of God. And the Spirit always says that which will win His approval—even when it alienates some men. Counselors must understand this. They are not to kowtow to counselees. When counselees mock God's word, when they make excuses for refusing to follow His ways, counselors can do nothing other than to assert the truth. It does not matter whether you "lose" them or not. If you trim the truth in order to win them, you will still lose them because they will not come to Christ on His terms. The problem is, you will also lose the genuine and sincere seekers after the truth who say, "Tell me more."

Peter then proceeded to tell them what the phenomenon they had experienced was all about. As he did so, he spoke in **revelatory words** (vv. 4, 14). The verb Luke used to describe Peter's preaching is *apophtheggomai*, an unusual term to the New Testament that appears only here and in Acts 26:25.[1] It was used by the Greeks to refer to the utterances of inspired prophets and similarly to prophetic address in the Septuagint.[2] The word often also indicates a clear, loud speech spoken under

---

[1] Where the source of Paul's words was challenged.

[2] Cf. I Chronicles 25:1; Zechariah 10:2; Ezekiel 13:9.

15   Certainly these people aren't drunk, as you imagine; it's only nine
        o'clock in the morning!

---

miraculous influence.[1] The point here is that this message (and those recorded hereafter[2]) was guided by the Spirit so as to convey precisely what He wanted the speaker to say. Timothy Dwight says, "Each inspired man was, as to his preaching, or his writing, absolutely preserved from error."[3]

Is this reading too much into a verb? Hardly. The Lord Jesus made it clear to His disciples on more than one occasion that He would send the Spirit to infallibly guide them as they spoke: **"Don't worry about what you will say in defense or how to do so, because the Holy Spirit will teach you in that very hour what you ought to say"** (Luke 12:11, 12). Again, consider these words: **"Get it settled in your hearts not to practice your defense beforehand because I will give you words and wisdom that none of your opponents will be able to withstand or contradict"** (Luke 21:14, 15; in this regard, cf. also Matthew 10:19, 20; Mark 13:11).[4] This is Luke's subtle, but incisive way of saying that these promises of the Savior were fulfilled, since he nowhere else commented on the fact.

Of what value is it to know that the sermons and speeches in Acts were inspired? It is of great value. If a preacher (or counselor) wishes to know what the Holy Spirit is concerned about in preaching and counseling, he can look at these promises and their fulfillment to discover where he should put the emphasis in his presentations. Moreover, an examination of these messages will provide much help in knowing how the Spirit

---

[1] For helpful discussions of the verb, see Vincent *Word Studies* on Acts 2:4; Girdlestone, *Old Testament Synonyms*; The *Expositor's Greek Testament* on Acts 26:25.

[2] Luke tells you something once and expects you will apply it thereafter. An example of this tendency is seen in his reference to the fact of abbreviation (v. 40), which is manifestly true of other addresses, but not mentioned subsequently. Here, the idea is that at the outset Luke tells us the sermons recorded in Acts are inspired.

[3] Sermon XLIX, Page 137.

For a very fine discussion of this matter, see J.M. Stifler, *An Introduction to the Study of the Book of the Acts of the Apostles*, Revell, N.Y., 1892, pp. 18-22.

[4] It is obvious from these two quotations that Luke was aware of Jesus' promise.

16   On the contrary, this is what the prophet Joel spoke about:

---

approaches people with biblical teaching.

Jesus said that He, through the Spirit, would provide four things, noted in the Gospel passages above. The Spirit would give them

- The Right Thing ("what" they would say)
- The Right Words ("how" they would say it)
- The Right Way ("wisdom" to say it well)
- The Right Time ("in that hour" appropriately applied)[1]

A good way to study each sermon and speech in Acts (as well as your own endeavors) is to run it through this four-item, analytical grid. If these things are the concerns expressed by the Holy Spirit, they ought also to be your concern in preaching and in counseling. This is true, especially, since you have no promise of inspired speech.

So, let's think of these four items in relationship to counseling for a moment (suggestively, not exhaustively). The *right thing* has to do with the content of what is said, the **what** in Luke 12:11 and 12. Here, of course, God expects those ministering in His Name to use the content that He has provided for them. Like Peter, the counselor ought to be able to apply biblical content to the existential situation: **this is what the prophet Joel spoke about** (v. 16). When a counselor cannot identify a counselee's problem by careful citation of biblical teaching there is something wrong. Of course, the counselee's problem may be organic, in which case the counselor may need to call on a physician for help. But if the problem is one that a counselor should rightly deal with, then he must be able to bring the correct Bible content to bear upon the issue. If he allows the problem to be framed in non-biblical, psychological jargon, he may fail to correctly identify it. Using biblical categories and biblical language is important so that the counselee views the problem in the light of what God has to say about it. Counselors must possess a wealth of biblical understanding and be able to locate appropriate Scripture to do this. As we shall see, they must be able to interpret these Scriptures properly as well.

The second concern of the Holy Spirit is *the right words*—the **how** mentioned in Luke 12. The words that one uses are significant. Words are not merely signs; they are also sign posts. Medical terms point to a physi-

---

[1] For more detail concerning these things see my book *Preaching According to the Holy Spirit*.

17   **In the last days, God says,**
       I will pour out My Spirit on all flesh,

---

cian for a solution; Psychological terms point to a shrink; only *biblical* terms point to Jesus Christ, Who is the solution to every counseling problem. Every counseling problem is a theological problem and, therefore, needs (and has) a theological solution. Non-theological solutions are not solutions. They are always something less than true solutions.

The third concern of the Spirit is *the right way.* The Spirit desires that the material be presented wisely; in Luke 21:14 and 15 Jesus emphasizes **wisdom**. Many counselors know what to say, and even may be quite eloquent in speaking truth from the Bible. But they may be unwise in the manner in which they present it. They may jump in when it is inappropriate to do so. They may become overbearing. They may be too anxious to help. If a counselor will study the Scriptures, looking for both precepts and examples, he will become wiser in this area, so long as he is open to criticism and change.

Lastly, the Holy Spirit is concerned about *the right time.* Jesus provided what was needed, in an appropriate manner (as Luke 12 indicates) precisely at the right time—**in that hour**. This element of timing may be closely associated with the last, but it also seems to have a place of its own. That which is timely may still be presented in an inappropriate manner that lacks wisdom. That which is spoken wisely, however, will usually be spoken in a timely way. There are those, however, who have difficulty knowing when, in a counseling situation, to bring up a particular matter. A biblical injunction, for instance, will not be received the same way when one is unaware of his need for it as when he is desperately seeking for a solution to that need.

Here, counselor, is a four item grid you can use to evaluate your counseling. Why not tape some sessions, then play them back studying the items that the Holy Spirit is concerned about? If you are one who is anxious to learn, you may improve greatly as a counselor in this way.

The passage Peter quoted from the prophet Joel was a direct forecast of the day of Pentecost and the **last days** of the Old Testament era (v. 17).[1] It foretold the **baptism** of the Spirit (1:5), Who was to be **poured out on all flesh** (v. 17). The Spirit's baptism would be poured out on all kinds of people (**all flesh**) so that various sorts of persons would be endowed with special gifts (cf. vv. 17, 18). This event heralded the new

---

[1] One reason that people have difficulty in interpreting prophecy correctly is that

13

and your sons and your daughters will prophesy,
your young men will see visions,
and your old men will dream dreams;

18   and even on My male and female slaves I will pour out My
Spirit in those days, and they will prophesy.

19   I will perform wonders in the sky above
and signs on the earth below—blood and fire and clouds of
smoke.

20   The sun will be darkened and the moon turned to blood
before the great and glorious day of the Lord comes.

21   Everybody who calls on the Lord's name will be saved.

22   Men of Israel, listen to these words: Jesus, the Nazarene, a Man
from God accredited to you by miracles and wonders and the
signs that God performed in your midst—as you yourselves
know—

---

era as well as ended the old. The new era would be a time when people
from all nations would be invited into the empire of Christ—and would
come! It would be a time when the old, exclusive Judaism would fold.
This latter overthrow of the old order was, in harmony with many prophetic passages in the Old Testament, signified by symbols indicating
great upheaval.[1] The seemingly unshakable would be shaken (vv. 19-20).
**The great and glorious day of the Lord, in which everybody who calls
on the Lord's name will be saved** had arrived, and Peter would be the
first to announce the good news (v. 21)!

Looking now at the message itself, we shall take time only to mention a few things. First, notice the purpose of the miracles (v. 22). They
were given to **accredit** Jesus Christ. Joel makes it clear that miracles were
to be confined to the last day period of 40 years, and thus have ceased.
There was no need for them following this period in which the new order
was established and the apostolic teaching was similarly accredited (cf.
II Corinthians 12:12; Hebrews 2:4). Counselees, confused about miracles,
should be carefully instructed about their purpose. Since we have that

---

they think every reference to last days or last times refers to the present era. In
actuality, it was the last days of Joel's era that was in view—the forty year transitional period that ended with the destruction of Jerusalem.

[1] Cf. Isaiah 2:12, 19; 13:10; 34:3, 4; 50:3; Jeremiah 4:23-26; Ezekiel 32:7, 8; Joel
3:14, 15; Hosea 10:8; Nahum 1:6. In these passages, none of which was to be
taken literally, predictions of the passing away of a seemingly unchangeable
order, like the seemingly unshakable elements, were set forth under these prophetic symbols.

23   this Man, delivered up by God's predetermined plan and fore-
knowledge, by the hands of lawless men, you killed by crucifix-
ion!

24   But God raised Him, releasing Him from the agonies of death,
because it wasn't possible for Him to be held by it.

25   This is true, because David says concerning Him,
I saw the Lord constantly in front of Me;
He is at My right hand, so that I won't be shaken.

26   **Because of this My heart was glad,**
and My tongue rejoiced;
My flesh also will live in hope,

27   **since You won't abandon My soul to the unseen world,**
or let Your Holy One see corruption.

28   **You have made life's ways known to Me;**
You will fill Me with gladness in Your presence.

---

which is complete in the Scriptures, there is no reason for miracles to occur; there is no prophet, apostle or Savior to authenticate!

The three words used in verse 22 are, **miracles**[1] (speaking of the nature of the act itself), **wonders** (speaking of the effect on those who observe the miracle) and **signs** (speaking of the purpose of the miracles). Often counselees who are in trouble are looking for miracles. When they reveal this penchant for miracles, make it clear to them that God initiated these miracles for His purposes (which we have just noted), and that miracles are not to be sought for any other. Too many (even otherwise biblical) counselors are loose about the language they use, calling extraordinary acts of providence miracles. It is wise to be careful about such things, so that counselees will not be misled. A healing may be an act of God's providence in answer to believing prayer, but it is not a miracle.

In verses 23 and 24 (as well as in 3:13; 4:26-28) predestination is solidly linked with human responsibility. The two should never be separated, even though some counselors wish to do so. Peter speaks about these matters to the Jews who needed to hear that these events were not a glitch in God's plan but, rather, precisely what He had ordered and predicted. Peter is straightforward about the sins of those who put Christ to death. Counselors who don't directly address the sin of counselees fail to bring the conviction that leads to repentance. You must learn to have the courage to speak the truth in love. Of course you must be sure that your counselees' actions are, without question, sinful before you confront them with their sin. Many counselors today—even those who are biblical in other

---

[1] Literally, "powers."

29 Brothers, I can tell you with confidence about the patriarch David, that he died and was buried, and his tomb is here with us to this day.

30 So then, being a prophet and knowing that **God had sworn to him with an oath that He would place one of his descendants on his throne,**

31 he foresaw and spoke about Christ's resurrection, that **He wasn't abandoned to the unseen world and that** His flesh **wouldn't see corruption.**

32 God raised up this Jesus—of this we all are witnesses.

33 Then, when He was exalted to God's right hand, He received the promised Holy Spirit from the Father and poured out this which you see and hear.

34 The fact is that David didn't ascend into the heavens, but he says,
**"The Lord said to my Lord,
Sit at My right hand**

35 **until I make Your enemies a stool for Your feet."**

36 So then, let the whole house of Israel know for certain that God has made this Jesus Whom you crucified both Lord and Christ.

---

regards—seem to be taking it on themselves to read the hearts of their counselees. Don't try. That is God's prerogative, not man's.

The Bible was also used in addressing those to whom it was an authoritative book. Counselors who fail to use Scripture with **confidence** (v. 29) as they apply it to the counseling situation, are making a serious mistake. Notice how Peter applies the passage from Joel to his hearers. In verses 32 and 33 he reverts to the passage, after quoting from the Psalms, once again emphasizing that the **promised** baptism of the Holy Spirit had taken place. This happened as the result of the **exaltation** of Jesus to the Father's **right hand**. His coming was in fulfillment of the prophecy, and thus indicated that Jesus had begun to reign as the God-man.[1] Now humanity had been exalted, in Him, to this high estate. Peter drives his point home in verse 36

After hearing this sermon, they wanted to know what they should do. That is the desire that both a preacher and a counselor wants to see in his listener. He is then on the threshold of change. Peter is clear—he doesn't leave it up to them to determine the next move (as some counselors do)—they must repent, believe the gospel and unite with Christ's church through baptism. They would be forgiven and would too receive the Holy

---

[1] As God, of course, He had never ceased to reign.

37 Now when they heard this, they were pierced to the heart and said to Peter and the rest of the apostles, "Brothers, what should we do?"

38 Peter said to them,

> Repent and be baptized, each one of you on the basis of the name of Jesus Christ for the forgiveness of your sins, and you will receive the gift of the Holy Spirit.

39   The promise is for you and your children and for all those who are at a distance, as many as the Lord may call.

40 And with many other words he solemnly gave testimony and urged them, saying, "Be saved from this twisted generation."

41 Then those who received his message were baptized, and about three thousand persons were added that day.

42 And they persevered in the apostles' teaching, in fellowship, in the breaking of bread and in prayer.

43 A sense of awe came over everybody. Many wonders and signs were done by the apostles,

44 and all who believed were together and had everything in common.

45 They sold their property and possessions and shared them with all, as any had need.

46 Every day they continued to meet in the temple in unity of spirit, and from house to house they broke bread together, sharing meals in gladness and sincerity of heart,

47 praising God and enjoying the favor of all the people. And day by day the Lord added to their number those who were being saved.

Spirit. This promise was to them, to their children, and to the Gentiles (v. 39)—**to as many as the Lord may call**.

Verse 40 indicates that Peter **urged** his hearers to take these actions. Many counselors (as well as preachers—especially of the extreme wing of the biblical-theological group) want to present the truth, then do nothing more. They will not encourage the listener to action. The failure is a notable one.

The results of the sermon were large (v. 41). And they were lasting (v. 42). When God truly does a work of grace in the human being, it is one that makes a difference; and it does not pass away. The spontaneous outcome of this remarkable change of regeneration is noted in verses 43 through 47.[1]

---

[1] Where the Spirit of God is at work in people the effect described in verses 46 and 47 will occur.

CHAPTER 3

1 Now Peter and John were going up to the temple at three o'clock in the afternoon, the hour of prayer.

2 And a certain man who was lame from birth was being carried to the temple gate called "Beautiful," where they used to put him every day so he could beg alms from those who entered the temple.

3 When he saw Peter and John about to enter the temple, he asked them to give him alms.

4 Peter and John stared at him and said, "Look at us."

5 He gave them his attention, expecting to get something from them.

As in the previous chapter, Peter's second recorded sermon was preached out of an event which, because of curiosity, brought together a crowd of listeners (3:1-11). To have hearers who are **filled with amazement and astonishment** is an ideal circumstance for preaching. A preacher seldom has it. Most preachers have to arouse interest in their subject and bring a congregation to the place where they are anxious to hear more. In both Acts 2 and 3, however, God prepared the audience for the message to come. The counselor has one great advantage over the preacher: usually his counselees are already tuned in to the problem that they will be discussing. Often they come quite desirous to hear. Of course, that is not always the case. Some are dragged into counseling by parents or by wives; others come only to prove to someone else that nothing can be done to rectify some bad situation. But for those who come for help, the counseling milieu into which counselor and counselee enter is ideal for the presentation of God's truth, which can lead to significant change.

Because this is so, it is sad when the counselor fails to take advantage of it, when he seeks to "build rapport" or does nothing more than listen, instead of bringing the Word of God to bear upon the problem. To do such things is to destroy an already advantageous situation. And, what is more, it amounts to a colossal failure to supply the revivifying water of the Word that alone quenches the thirst of parched souls.

First, consider the miracle. When the beggar asks for alms, Peter does not hesitate. He knows what he has and offers it: **I don't have any silver or gold, but what I do have I will give you. In the name of Jesus Christ the Nazarene, walk** (v. 6). This was a notable miracle. Everyone knew this man (v. 10) and that he had been lame from birth (v. 2). They

6   Peter said, "I don't have any silver or gold, but what I do have I will give you: In the name of Jesus Christ the Nazarene, walk!"

7   Then taking him by the right hand, he helped him up, and at once his feet and ankles were strengthened,

8   and jumping up, he stood and walked and went into the temple grounds with them, walking and jumping and praising God.

9   The people saw him walking and praising God,

10   and they recognized him as the one who sat begging for alms at the Beautiful gate of the temple. So they were filled with amazement and astonishment at what had happened to him.

11 As he clung to Peter and John, all the people were amazed and ran together to them at the portico called "Solomon's."

12   When he saw this, Peter answered the people,

---

could not help but be impressed. Your counselee may come wanting *one* thing—relief, psychological evaluation or some pragmatic answer to a problem—but if you are a biblical counselor you know what you have to offer him. You know that you possess something greater than what the person is asking for, that will meet a deeper need in his life. You, like Peter, should not hesitate to say (in effect), "I don't have psychology or good advice, but what I do have I will give you." Then, in a non-miraculous way, you should proceed to offer the help that is found in the Bible. And, note, also, how Peter does not allow the man to think that this power to heal him lies in himself; rather, he explicitly commands him to walk *in the name of Jesus Christ*. You too, from the outset, must make it clear that your wisdom and techniques will not solve his problem; what you bring to the counseling situation is the Word of Christ, and (indeed) the power of Christ through the Spirit Himself as He works in and through that Word. Counselees need to know up front, who is involved in the counseling transaction—that it is not merely you and they, but also a Third Party Who is the All-important One. Tell them that, ultimately, it is He with Whom they have to do. You are, as Peter was, but His servant, ministering His Word. The change that occurs, if any proper change does, will be brought about by His power. Christ is at work in biblical counseling.

Then, comes the ensuing message to the crowd (vv. 12-26). The interesting way in which it is introduced is this: **Peter answered the people** (v. 12). Every counseling situation, like every sermon, ought to be an **answer**. Peter knew what they were thinking. He read his audience and

Men of Israel, why are you surprised at this? Why do you stare at us as though by our own power or piety we had made him walk?

13   The God of Abraham, Isaac and Jacob, the God of our fathers, glorified His Servant Jesus, Whom you delivered up and denied in front of Pilate when he had decided to free Him.

14   But you denied the Holy and Righteous One and asked for a murderer to be given to you.

15   So you killed the Author of life, Whom God raised from the dead, to which fact we are witnesses.

---

answered the question that was uppermost in their minds—"How did Peter do this?" A counseling session, like a sermon, really doesn't even begin until it becomes an answer. The answer will not always (even usually) be the one that a person thinks he will receive, but it ought to be addressed to a question. Most counselees, as I said, come already filled with questions. Your task, like Peter's was, is to help frame the counselees' questions according to biblical parameters in order to direct those questions into channels that fit the answers found in the Scriptures. That will often take some time and effort.[1]

Notice how Peter begins at exactly that point. He says, **"why are you surprised at this? Why do you stare at us as though by our own power or piety we had made him walk? The God of Abraham. . . ."** Peter must turn the concern of his audience away from himself toward God and Christ. That, as I said above, is one of the principal tasks that you have at the outset of every counseling case. People will be oriented toward their problems and toward you. They must be shown that in biblical counseling there is a different orientation altogether.

Peter once more uses his message to link Jesus with his congregation's heritage derived from the Patriarchs, to show that Jesus' death was but the fulfillment of all they had looked forward to. He quickly moves to the event that made the healing possible—the substitutionary death of Christ on the cross and His subsequent resurrection.[2] But again we see Peter driving home the fact of their sin and their need for **repentance** (vv.

---

[1] One way to accomplish this is, like Peter, to begin framing your answer in the form of rhetorical questions (v. 12). Jesus often answered questions with further questions. This helps counselees to think more clearly, suggests possibilities (and impossibilities) that he needs to consider and turns his thinking in desired directions. Peter expects no answer to his questions; but he does expect thought to ensue.

16   But on the basis of faith in His name this man, whom you see and know, has been strengthened, and faith in Him has given him this perfectly sound body in the presence of all of you.
  17 Now, brothers, I know that you acted in ignorance, the same as your rulers did.
18   But what God foretold by the mouth of all the prophets, that His Christ was to suffer, He fulfilled in this way.

12-15, 19), while at the same time making it clear that it was this same Jesus Whom they had rejected Who had performed the healing (vv. 13-16). The continued emphasis on Jesus as the One behind everything is the true answer to their questions. That, too, is what you must emphasize in counseling. What you want to do is to help your counselee build rapport with Jesus Christ!

In this presentation of the truth, remember, the Holy Spirit guided Peter into these channels. We must never forget this; Peter said the right words, wisely presented at the right time to teach the right thing. And even on this informal occasion, the form of the sermon was that of a *logos*. It began with the words, **Men of Israel** (v. 12), which was the standard speech form of the day used to introduce a *logos* (or formal sermon or speech). Throughout the book of Acts we find the Holy Spirit using this form. It is therefore important to note that the Spirit did not inspire mere responses, but carefully constructed ones that observed the speaking conventions of the times. Our counseling ought not consist of offhand utterances, but of carefully considered responses. We must strive to present things precisely and clearly. Too few counselors take the time to work on their manner of presentation, the words they use, or the time in which they present truth. There is a slipshod way of doing things and a careful way. The biblical counselor must always work on improving his approaches.

It is interesting how Peter moves to direct biblical support for what he is saying only at the end of his message (vv. 22ff.). Often, the use of the Bible should be postponed until such a time as you have oriented the listener to the particular passages of Scripture to which you plan to refer. Otherwise, he may not appreciate the teaching of those passages and will wonder why you are referring to them. Peter had mentioned that what

---

[2] In Acts Luke always coupled the cross with the resurrection (as Paul did in I Corinthians 15:1ff.) when summarizing the gospel. There is no salvation apart from a risen Savior.

19	So then, repent and turn around that your sins might be wiped out,
20	that times of refreshing may come from the presence of the Lord, and He may send Jesus, the Christ Who was appointed for you beforehand.
21	Heaven had to receive Him until the times when everything was to be restored, of which God spoke through the mouth of His holy prophets from ages past.
22	Indeed, Moses said, **"The Lord God will raise up a Prophet for you from among your brothers, just like me. You must listen to whatever He tells you.**
23	**Any person who doesn't listen to that Prophet will be cut off entirely from the people."**
24	And all the prophets from Samuel and those who came afterward, as many as spoke, also announced these days.
25	You are the sons of the prophets and of the covenant that God made with our fathers, saying to Abraham, **"And in your descendants all the families of the earth will be blessed."**

happened to Jesus was according to prophecy (vv. 18, 21), but had not yet shown how this is so. Often counselors shove a Bible verse into the face of a counselee before preparing him to receive and understand it. Build up to biblical truth by first relating it to the counselee in his situation. That doesn't mean waiting for several sessions before you turn to Scripture. But it does mean, in one session, working your way up to the biblical truth by laying a groundwork for it and showing how it relates to the problem at hand. Then, it is also necessary to explicate and apply it. That brings the Bible home to the counselee with greater force.

The emphasis, when Peter does turn to Scripture, is on Christ's *words*: **You must listen to whatever He tells you** (v. 22). That ought to be your emphasis in counseling. In this and the following verses he says:
- Christ's words are a must (v. 22)
- Christ's words are a threat (v. 23)
- Christ's words are a certainty (vv. 24, 25)
- Christ's words are a blessing (v. 25).

This outline of the biblical passages is one that might be used profitably in many counseling sessions. Note especially the climax: Christ is a **blessing** to those who **turn from their wicked ways**. That isn't the way many counselors speak of Jesus Christ today. "Christian counselors," who are not particularly biblical in their approach, often hold out Jesus as a blessing to *add on* to one's life. Quite to the contrary, He is a blessing to those

26   God raised up His Servant and sent Him to you first, to bless you
       by turning each one of you from your wicked ways.

---

who are willing to have Him upset their entire lifestyle. They must **turn**[1]
from sin to righteousness.

There is much more in this message that could be explored (I hope
you will do so), but for our purposes we shall press forward.

---

[1] *Shuv*, "to turn," is the Hebrew word for repentance. It means a change of mind
that leads to a change of life. Those who heard Peter understood the expression to
mean that.

CHAPTER 4

1 While they were speaking to the people, the priests and captain of
the temple guard and the Sadducees came up to them,
2   annoyed because they were teaching the people and announcing the
resurrection of the dead by Jesus.
3   So they arrested them, and because it was evening, they took them in
custody till the next day.
4   But many of those who heard the message believed, and the number of
the men came to about five thousand.

The proclamation of the truth in power (cf. 1:8) often does not satisfy
the guardians of political or religious power. The Sanhedrin was both
political and religious. The apostles were **arrested** for preaching the gospel (vv. 1, 2). Nobody said that ministry was a cinch. Before He left them,
Jesus told the disciples that they would undergo persecution of all sorts.
But that was not the case only for the disciples; it has been true down
through history for leaders and laity alike, and is no less true today. But
those who minister in Christ's Name especially must be prepared to
endure taunts, scorn and persecution from those who oppose God's truth.
Even within the church there is often a bias against the Bible. Christians
who want to be accepted by the world so as to get along with them, will
often take up the cudgels against fellow believers who wish to be biblical.
They can become viciously critical of other Christians when they expose
error and compromise.

The apostles were arrested because of the message they preached:
**they were teaching the people and announcing the resurrection of the
dead by Jesus.** This **annoyed** the Sadducees for two reasons, who were
in ascendancy among the members of the religio-political leadership of
Israel. The Sadducees did not believe in the **resurrection** of the dead—
indeed, as we shall see in a later chapter of Acts, they were likely to get
very upset whenever this doctrine was affirmed. Secondly, they bore a
large share of the responsibility for putting Jesus to death. The truth that
He had now risen from the dead was a truth they didn't want to hear. It ran
contrary to everything they had hoped to accomplish by His death. So,
both for doctrinal reasons and because they did not want to face the fact of
the resurrection, they immediately determined to eliminate any further
threat by imprisoning those who were teaching about Jesus and the resurrection.

But before they were able to curtail the apostles' preaching, we are

5 Now the next day their rulers, elders and scribes were gathered together in Jerusalem

6 together with Annas, the high priest, Caiaphas, John, Alexander and all who belonged to the high-priestly order.

7 And they stood them in the midst and asked, "By what power or in what name did you do this?"

---

told that 5,000 men (how many women and children we are not told) **believed** their message. The rulers could see that the church was rapidly gaining momentum, and they feared it. People who resist truth always fear those who present it. That is true whether we are talking about a counselee who will not face up to the facts about a wife who has left him, or whether we are talking about a counselor who is challenged to consider giving up his psychological props and instead rest in the Word and power of God. A common reaction to fear is to try to eliminate the source of fear—and this often reaches extreme lengths. Just be aware of it. It is not uncommon. Understand that people who are bent on securing themselves from anything that might upset their comfortable situations may take desperate actions. Don't be surprised when it happens as the result of successful counseling.

The next day an informal hearing took place (vv. 5-7). All the notables of the community gathered to look into the matter of this preaching and the movement which seemed to be growing out of nowhere. They questioned the preachers: **by what power or in what name did you do this?** They wanted to know the source of their authority for healing and teaching, and whether what they had heard them say about Jesus was truly what they had taught (cf.3:7[b]). Once more, Peter, **filled with the Holy Spirit,**[1] stepped forward to speak (v. 8ff.). Those who preach Christ are often afforded important opportunities to give a witness for Him in the most unexpected places, even through the very opposition that their preaching provokes. This also is true, as many biblical counselors will tell you, for those who stand on the Scriptures as the sole basis for their counseling. Do your work for Him well, become an expert in it, and in one way or another (there are not many kings around any more!) watch God fulfill the promise of Proverbs 22:29.

---

[1] Doubtless an example of the way in which Jesus' prophecy about **power** (recorded in 1:8) was fulfilled. And in the case of an apostle, as we have seen, this filling of the Spirit included the ability to speak revelatory words without previous preparation.

8   Then Peter, filled with the Holy Spirit, said to them,
          Rulers of the people and elders—
9   If we are being examined today about a good deed done to a sick
          person, about how he was healed,
10   let all of you and all of the people of Israel know that it is by the
          name of Jesus Christ the Nazarene, Whom you crucified, Whom
          God raised from the dead, by Him this person stands before you a
          well man.

Peter addressed the august body, using the designations that fit them (v. 8). His brief speech (it may have been abbreviated by Luke so as to give us but the gist of it) once again focused on their sin in putting Jesus to **death**, His subsequent **resurrection**, the prophecy-fulfilling nature of what had happened, and the fact that **salvation** is through His **Name** alone (vv. 11, 12). They had asked about the **name** (authority) by which the healing had taken place. Peter made it abundantly clear that it was in the Name of Jesus that the cripple was healed, and moreover, that it is in that Name alone, of all the names in the world, that one can find salvation. He took up their question and used it as a springboard to drive home the need to trust Christ as Savior. The name Jesus, of course, means "Yahweh saves." It was given to Him at His birth by an angel who told Joseph that He should be called "Jesus" *because He would save His people from their sins.* Clearly, it is that thought Peter was getting at.

It is always a good procedure in counseling to take the words, phrases and ideas expressed by a counselee and enlarge on or otherwise use them to make a biblical point. What you have done, in effect, is to attach your point to something already in his mind. That makes it easier for him to remember it in the future, as well as see the relationship it bears to his thinking in the present. Take a trivial example. A counselee says, "I'm fed up with the attitude that Bob has been taking." You might respond, "Really. How fed up are you with the Word of God that will enable you to do good to Bob when he despitefully uses you? You should be fed up to the full with good things from God so that you will not become fed up with others."

When Peter, speaking of the risen Jesus, said, **by Him this person stands before you a well man** (v. 10^b), he was answering the second half of their question; the question concerned the name (authority) and the **power** by which the miracle was performed. Once more this healing must have enraged the rulers. They thought that their power, exerted against Jesus, had vanquished Him. Now, as a risen Savior, His power was being

11   He is the **Stone rejected** by you **builders, Who has become the Head of the corner**.

12   There is salvation by nobody else, since there is no other name beneath the sky that has been given by human beings by which we must be saved.

13 Now when they saw the boldness of Peter and John and realized that they were uneducated laymen, they were surprised and recognized that they had been with Jesus.

---

exerted once again through Galilean *fisherman* (of all things) to heal in their very midst! God has a way of taking that which is feeble, weak, and of no account to the world and using it to manifest the power of Jesus Christ (cf. I Corinthians 1:26-29). In counseling this happens all the time. People who have not been helped substantially by psychiatrists and psychologists find genuine, lasting solutions to their problems by consulting with simple, Bible-believing counselors who rely upon the Scriptures. This often enrages those whose methods fail and causes them to scorn or even slander the one who has helped another. It is interesting to observe that the emphasis wasn't placed on the help that the lame man received by the power of Christ through the ministry of Jesus. Rather, the emphasis was on the one ministering and whether or not he conformed to the accepted rules and regulations. Similarly today, concern may not be shown for the welfare of the poor counselee who is helped, but about the counselor (on whom opprobrium is heaped) who dared to restrict his help to that which he found in the Bible. He wasn't kosher!

Verse 13 is noteworthy. Those who walk with Jesus *become* like Him. In Luke 6:40, Jesus set forth His philosophy of education. A student isn't above his teacher; but when that student is thoroughly trained, he will become like his teacher. Notice He did not say he will *think like* his teacher. He said will *be like* him. Jesus took twelve men to live with Him for three and a half years so that they could become like Him. Then after that time of training, others **recognized that they had been with Jesus.** In this process we see the fundamental principle of discipleship—the "with him" principle.[1] People become like those with whom they closely associate. That is why it is so important to choose one's associates carefully (cf. I Corinthians 15:33). We all imitate others. Often, perhaps most often, we do so unconsciously, not realizing how much we absorb from being with them. Imitation is a doctrine that runs all through the New Tes-

---

[1] Cf. Mark 3:14. Pointed out to me by Ken Smith.

14 But seeing the man who had been healed standing with them, they had nothing to say in opposition.

15 So they ordered them to leave the meeting of the Sanhedrin and discussed the matter with one another.

---

tament. Paul, for instance, commands, "Be imitators of me as I am an imitator of Christ" (I Corinthians 11:1). Counselors should take advantage of the fact that we learn many of our ways by imitation. They should help counselees to cement relationships with those who could impart much to them through the process. As an adjunct to verbal counsel, imitation of those who are living well for Christ is probably the one single thing most likely to help counselees. Counselors should remember that the more time counselees spend with them, the more they are likely to become like their counselors. Are you ready for others to imitate you? Should they?

Peter's **boldness** stood out to the rulers. The word "boldness"[1] is an important one that we shall encounter more than once as we continue to study Acts. It is a term that has largely to do with boldness of speech. It means "to speak forthrightly without fear of consequences." Of course, that is precisely what Jesus did. Afterward His former disciples acted exactly like Him! And what Peter did was not in accord with his background as a fisherman. He had not been trained in the schools. He had not taken courses in rhetoric. Prior to Pentecost, he had not become a spokesman for any cause. Yet, here he was speaking boldly for Jesus and Christianity with power and persuasion so that thousands assented. The rulers were taken by **surprise**, Luke says, probably since Peter and John were **uneducated laymen** from whom you would hardly expect such bold, convincing speech (v. 13).

The healing, however, created quite a problem for the rulers. The presence of the healed man stopped them in their tracks and seemed to stop their mouths as well (v. 14). So they lamely dismissed them while they **discussed** what to do (v. 15). It was not merely Peter and John and the healed man with whom they had to reckon. Nor was it merely the 120 people that had been present on the day of Pentecost. There were now crowds of followers who had professed faith in Jesus Christ, probably as many as 10,000. It was a movement that they had to face up to—a movement that had sprung up overnight. And it was not like the movement spawned by John the Baptist, that had no organization associated with it. Here was a full blown "church," developing officers, a membership, and

---

[1] Not the word for boldness that means "daring."

16	They said,

> What are we going to do with these people? That a notable sign has taken place through them is apparent to everybody living in Jerusalem, and we can't deny it.

17	But to keep this from spreading further among the people, let's warn them not to speak in this name any longer to anybody.

18	So they called them and ordered them not to teach or offer a word in Jesus' name.

19	But Peter and John replied by saying,

> If it is right before God to listen to you rather than God, you decide.

20	We can't do anything but speak what we saw and heard.

---

holding regular meetings. That signaled permanence. They said, "**What are we going to do with these people?**" (v. 16). They had to confess that a **notable sign** had taken place. If they wanted to hold their present places and positions, they would have to do something to contend with the movement that had mushroomed all around them; otherwise it would **spread** (v. 17).

Finally, the rulers determined to **warn the apostles** not to speak in Christ's name again (v. 18). Accordingly, they **called them** and issued the warning. But Peter's boldness again emerged. He replied saying, "**If it is right before God to listen to you rather than God, you decide. We can't do anything but speak what we saw and heard.**" How magnificent! This statement stands side by side with Luther's great declaration at the Diet of Worms.

We need preachers and counselors today who will stand firmly and say similar things in response to the pressures (and sometimes warnings) of those who would overthrow biblical counseling. The very essence of true discipleship is summed up in those words: we spoke **what we saw and heard**. That was the way in which Jesus described discipleship in relationship to His Father (cf. John 8:28; 3:32). That is the essence of what is needed in counseling. As I said earlier in the chapter, **seeing** (so that one may imitate) is as crucial as **hearing.** Both are needed; without the one or the other, something vital is missing. It is important in counseling not to depend solely on what is done in the counseling room—where people talk—but to observe real life decision-making on the part of other Christians who in their everyday activities use those principles a counselee is learning in counseling. Counselors must evaluate the resources that they have available in their congregations, enlist people to whom they can send counselees for such purposes and develop ways and means of

21 So when they had threatened them further, they released them. They couldn't find a way to punish them because of the people; everybody was praising God for what had happened.

22 The fact is that the man on whom this sign of healing was performed was more than forty years old.

23 Now when they were released, they went to their own friends and told them what the chief priests and elders had said to them.

---

prying counseling loose from the stogy, abstract setting that may develop when principles fail to get coupled with life. Each counselor should spend the time required to find ways in the milieus in which he and his counselees live to make such real life settings available for counselees.

Relying on their **threats**, (at this moment they feared the crowd to do anything more) the Sanhedrin let the disciples go. They were still bent on punishing them, however, but they determined to bide their time until they could think of ways to do so that would not lead to retaliation on the part of the crowd that seemed to be decidedly in favor of the imprisoned preachers (v. 21). Luke, as physician, notes that the man who had been healed was more than forty years of age. All those years he had borne that affliction. In no way was it possible that he would have simply sprung out of his illness on his own (vs. 22).

The weakness of those who know they are in the wrong is apparent. It is this same thing we are beginning to see more and more as those who are addicted to non-biblical counseling begin to take note of the swelling movement toward biblical counseling that is growing up all over the country. Ignoring it has done no good. Warning against it has not succeeded very well either. One wonders what behind the scene discussions that those who are threatened by this movement engage in. Are they thinking up ways to punish biblical counselors for asserting their Scriptural rights? Will they take action in the future against them, as we shall see that these rulers did? Those are questions to ponder.

The apostles returned to their **friends** (the others were anything but friends; they had made themselves enemies of the apostles). Perhaps a word needs to be added here about this matter. Biblical counselors are not enemies of those who have been immersed in non-biblical counseling. Many of these persons—especially believers—had good motives in entering the field (they wanted to help people). But they were sold a bill of goods. Now, when they see increasingly that so few are helped, and they investigate and see that biblical counseling helps so many, they face a dilemma. They have a deep investment in years of training, have written articles and follow practices which they would have to repudiate and abandon to change to biblical counseling. So, at best, many temporize ("The Bible can do some things—perhaps more than we thought—but not everything. There is still a legitimate place for psychological counseling"[1]). But others, like these rulers, know that they have been challenged and look for a way in which to fight back—in their minds they have made biblical counselors *the enemy*.

So far as biblical counselors are concerned, they are looking for many of those who profess faith in Christ, and who sincerely care about helping people, to eventually come over into their fold. They see in many Sauls, potential Pauls. Should they change allegiance, they would be surprised at the ready welcome they would receive. Biblical counselors don't look at their brothers who are duped by psychological claims as enemies. Indeed, they look on them as saints in error. They are awaiting the Spirit to convince them by the Scriptures that they should become biblical. Biblical counselors want to be friends—even now, when there is so much difference. They welcome dialog. They want opportunities, like the one Peter took advantage of before the Sanhedrin, to speak the truth boldly, hoping God will produce fruit among them.

Biblical counselors can envision the plight of the non-biblical Christian counselor. They see him in consternation over the biblical counseling movement. "Why won't it go away? What, really, is there to it? Notable achievements have occurred. How come? What should be my relationship to it?" Persons facing these questions are vulnerable because they know that their own position is so unstable. Non-biblical counselors are like the **double-minded** people described by James; they are **unstable in all their ways**. Psychological counselors cannot be otherwise, if they possess a modicum of honesty. They know that there are (literally) hundreds of contesting counseling views in the marketplace. If they are solidly anchored to any one of them, this is because they lack a proper appreciation of the situation. Again and again studies have shown that no one system out there has proven itself superior to the others. Studies also show that the spontaneous remission rate is as good or better than the results obtained from most of these systems! Moreover, new systems come and go so rapidly that a counselor caught in the current of this stream of viewpoints (to change the metaphor in mid stream!) finds that every five years or so he must retool. That becomes discouraging after a while. It should alert him

---

[1] I would like to see a biblical argument that there is such a place. So far it is non-existent.

24 When they heard it, as one they lifted their voices to God and said,
   **Sovereign Lord, Who made the sky and the earth and the sea,
   and all that is in them;**

25 Who from the mouth of our father David by the Holy Spirit said,
   **Why did the Gentiles rage
   and the people devise empty stratagems?**

26 **The kings of the earth took a belligerent stand,
   and the rulers gathered together against the Lord
   and against His Christ—**

27 In this city it is true that Herod and Pontius Pilate together with
   the Gentiles and people of Israel gathered together against Your
   holy Servant Jesus, Whom You anointed

28 to do those things that Your hand and Your plan had predestined
   to take place.

29 So now, Lord, take note of their threats and give Your slaves all
   the boldness needed to speak Your word.

30 Stretch out Your hand to heal and perform signs and wonders by
   the name of Your holy Servant Jesus.

---

to question all the claims. Who is right? Who has the time or wisdom to study all the offerings that come floating downstream and determine which, if any, or which parts of each (if any), are to be rejected and which are to be retained?

Biblical counselors are aware of these problems faced by so many of their brothers in Christ and urge them to step out of the stream (into which, as the philosopher said, one never steps twice) onto solid ground. All is *not in* flux (contrary to what he also said). Don't become resigned to that idea. There is something firm and unshakable—the Word of the Lord which stands forever.

In the prayer that follows (vv. 24-31), they quoted Scripture relating to the recent events of the death and resurrection of Jesus Christ. Their words (vv. 27, 28) indicated a perfect understanding of the meaning of the prophecies quoted. The events squared precisely with what was predicted. But then a twofold request is made:

First, since the rulers had **threatened** them, and since they intended to obey the Lord rather than them, they asked the Lord to please take note of those threats and keep them from backing down. They asked the Lord to instead give them the necessary **boldness** (same word as in v. 13) **needed to speak the word**. Boldness is essential to preaching (and counseling) from the Word. Have you prayed for boldness to minister in these ways? If not, you had better do so. Read again Ephesians 6:20. There, Paul, speak-

31 Now as they were praying, the place where they were meeting was shaken and they were all filled with the Holy Spirit and spoke God's word boldly.

32 Now the whole company of those who believed was of one heart and soul, and nobody said that his possessions were his own; instead, they used everything in common.

33 The apostles gave their testimony about the resurrection of the Lord Jesus with great power, and much grace was on all of them.

34 There wasn't a needy person among them. Whoever owned lands or houses sold them and brought the proceeds of what was sold

35 and placed them at the apostles' feet, and it was distributed to each as he had need.

36 Now Joseph, a Levite and native Cypriot, to whom the apostles gave the name Barnabas (which, translated, means "son of encouragement"),

37 sold a field that belonged to him and brought the money and placed it at the apostles' feet.

---

ing like Peter, says that this boldness to speak **ought to** characterize his ministry and he asks his readers to pray that he will maintain it.

Second, the other request they make is that God will continue to manifest Himself through their ministries. They wanted Jesus to continue to do what He had so recently done for this lame man. Prayer for God's continued use of your ministry is, therefore, essential. Christ provides the incentives, the wisdom and the power (cf. Philippians 2:13) for everything worthwhile that is accomplished in His kingdom. And those things come by prayer. To Him belongs all the glory!

Their prayer was answered (v. 31). The Spirit filled them all and they spoke God's word boldly. This filling was manifested in the sharing that voluntarily accompanied the Spirit's work (vv. 32-34[a]). They sold property and brought the proceeds to the apostles (v. 34). There was no coercion in any of this (5:4 makes this abundantly clear). There was no communism involved. It was something they did under circumstances where many had become deprived of livelihoods by their profession of faith in Christ (we later read of the "poor at Jerusalem"). In this temporary situation this emergency measure met their immediate needs (v. 34). But even under those ideal conditions (cf. v. 32) sin manifested itself, as we shall see in the next chapter. We also notice that Joseph, to whom the apostles gave the name Barnabas (**son of encouragement**), because he was an encourager, was one of those involved in earnestly seeking to help those who suffered. Barnabas also later plays a prominent part in helping Paul launch and pursue his early ministry.

CHAPTER 5

1 But a man named Ananias, together with his wife Sapphira, sold a
piece of property
2 and (with his wife's knowledge) kept a part of the sale price for himself and brought the rest and placed it at the apostles' feet.
3 But Peter said,
> Why has Satan filled your heart to lie to the Holy Spirit and keep
> a part of the receipts from the sale of the land for yourself?

This long chapter teaches the counselor many things—if he only has
the eyes to see them. **A man named Ananias** is how it begins. Notice
Luke's careful wording: he doesn't say "a *brother* named Ananias" or "a
disciple named Ananias." Presumably, as in the Old Testament "mixed
multitude," the wheat and tares Jesus anticipated in His parable began to
appear from the beginning. Ananias and his wife Sapphira were the first
observable instance of this reality. They wanted to be thought of as part of
those who contributed all that they had—even though there was no com-
pulsion upon them to sell or give. The fact is that they were more interested in what others thought than in helping the needy. In addition, they
skimmed off enough money from the sale to squirrel away a tidy sum for
safe keeping. They represented what they brought, like the others who
genuinely did so, as the full sale price obtained.

Peter, through the divine gift of discernment given to the apostles in
the days before the destruction of Jerusalem, saw through the deception.
He said that **Satan** had **filled** Ananias' **heart to lie to the Holy Spirit**.
Satan was already attempting to sow darnel seeds (tares) among the members of the church. If the **filling** of the **heart** by **Satan** was a direct,
unmeditated thing, then it is further evidence that Ananias was not a
believer. Satan doesn't fill the heart of one whose heart is already filled
with the Holy Spirit. And John made it clear that Satan cannot even **touch**
the believer (I John 5:18). It is important to make it clear to a counselee
that Satan is a defeated foe (see Colossians 2) and that he has no power to
directly influence him. When he sins, therefore, he can blame it on no one
but himself. But, on the other hand, that means that since he is not in the
clutches of some outside force, he is capable of changing his behavior by
the power of the Word and the Spirit. That is good news. Avoid teaching
that claims more for Satan than the Scriptures indicate he is capable of
doing.

The Holy Spirit was the One working in and through the church. A

4   While it was still yours, you could have kept it, couldn't you? And after it was sold, wasn't it yours to do with as you wished? How could you contrive such a thing in your heart? You haven't lied to men; no, you lied to God!

5   When Ananias heard these words, he fell down and died, and great fear came upon all who heard.

6   The young men got up, wrapped him up, carried him out and buried him.

---

lie to the apostles, who represented Him, was therefore a lie to the Spirit.[1] Ananias' possessions were his at every point (v. 4). Even the sum of money he had from the sale was still considered his until given away. There was no communism here. Lies and misrepresentations are to be expected from unbelievers. They are of their father the devil who is a liar and the father of lies (John 8:44).

According to verse 5, God took his life. This event, (like the event in the early history of the people of Israel in which a man was put to death for picking up sticks on the Sabbath) showed everyone from the outset that God means business. Good teachers understand this. At the beginning of each school year they come down hard on infractions of rules to show the class *they* mean business. Counselors also quickly learn they must do the same. If, for instance, a counselee does his homework poorly (or not at all) and having discerned that there is no valid reason for this, a wise counselor will bring counseling to a screeching halt saying something like, "This is a serious matter. You tell me you want to do what God requires, yet look at what you brought to the session this week! Do you think that is worthy of Him? We cannot go on in counseling until you do the assignment properly. So, for the rest of the session I shall simply read a book (or do whatever is at hand) while you are in the next room completing it." If there is resistance, the counselor will tell the counselee that the next session will begin only when the counselee brings the completed assignment with him. Doing this early on assures a number of things. If the person is insincere, he will leave counseling. That is important to know so that you don't waste time with him—there are others who could use the counseling hour profitably. Or, if he is genuine at heart, but sloppy in practice, this should stiffen him up a bit, and you should get better results from then on. Indeed, it may be the first stage in teaching him

---

[1] Incidentally, a proof for the deity of the Spirit is the identification of Him with God (vv. 3, 4). To lie to the Spirit is to lie to God.

7   About three hours later his wife came in, not knowing what had happened.

8   And Peter said to her, "Tell me whether you sold the land for such and such an amount." And she said, "Yes, for such and such an amount."

9   Then Peter said to her,

> Why have you two agreed to put the Lord's Spirit to the test? See, the feet of those who buried your husband are at the door, and they will carry you out.

10   Instantly she fell down at his feet and died. When the young men came in, they found her dead and carried her out and buried her beside her husband.

11   Great fear came over the whole church and over all who heard these things.

---

some discipline. He will need discipline to effect the new patterns that God requires of him.

Ananias' wife Sapphira also lied—and died (vv. 5-10)! The result was that **great fear came upon the whole church and all those who heard** (vv. 5, 11). There ought to be fear within and without the church when men contemplate the great God Whom they have offended by their disobedience. One of the problems with our society today is that there is little or no fear of God. When the churches stopped preaching about hell and the holiness of God, that was one major result. How many counselors mention the judgment, the eternal wrath of God, or even the judgments of God upon us in this life (I Corinthians 11:29-32)? The answer, sad to say, is *all too few*. We have overstressed the fact that, for Christians, **fear** means reverential awe. While that may be true in some instances (perhaps many) of the word's use it is not the only nuance to be noted. Here, as elsewhere, the word refers to a dread of the holiness of God which, when violated, leads to judgment. Fear should come even upon us as His children (note how fear came upon the **whole church**, not just unbelievers). While there is to be loving trust, there is also a certain fear that every disobedient child should have for his earthly parent. The same is true of trusting, but fearing, the heavenly Father. Since that notion runs contrary to the prevailing "wisdom" of our day, it is no longer stressed in churches which are strongly influenced by the world. The word **fear** (and the concept that it used to convey) has been so neutralized, that it no longer has even the slightest bite. But we see that God's swift action through Peter brought fear of God's holiness and power—honest-to-goodness *fear*—to everyone, believer and unbeliever alike!

12 Now many signs and wonders were performed among the people by the hands of the apostles. And they all used to meet with one mind in Solomon's portico.

13 But the rest didn't dare to join them; yet the people spoke highly of them,

14 and more than ever believers were added to the Lord, great throngs of men and women.

15 They actually brought the sick out into the streets and put them on beds and mats, so that as Peter went by his shadow might fall on some of them.

16 A crowd also came together from the cities round about Jerusalem, bringing the sick and those who were tormented by unclean spirits, and they were all healed.

17 But the high priest, and all those who were with him (who were of the sect of the Sadducees), filled with jealousy, rose up

---

In spite of threats by the officials, the apostles continued to teach and heal and meet together with the members of the church at Solomon's portico (v. 12). The **rest** mentioned in verse 13 probably refers to those who **heard** (the people of v. 12) but who were not members of the church (v. 11). Their fear of God, interestingly enough, did not drive people away from their teaching but was an attraction. They didn't reason the way that some Christians reason today—that preaching the wrath and judgment of God upon unrepentant sinners would repel people. Instead, they preached boldly, and people were drawn to the apostles' teaching. Who wants to worship and serve a god who is a pushover? Many people, while not becoming members of the church, seemed fascinated by what the apostles were doing and **spoke highly of them** (v. 13). Though this was the general response, there were, in addition, many who did **join them;** there were **added** to the church **great throngs of men and women**. This is another snapshot of the enormous growth of the early church in Jerusalem. Jesus' prayer from the cross[1] was being fulfilled. People, as they did when Jesus had taught and healed, also came bringing their sick (vv. 15, 16). Indeed, as the word got out, people began coming even from a distance. And God **healed** them **all** (v. 16).

Things went from bad to worse, as the rulers saw it. Now, with enormous crowds thronging Peter and the apostles, the High Priest and the Sadducees were **filled with jealousy**. Here is another problem that runs

---

[1] "Father, forgive them." The prayer was fulfilled when people heard the message, repented, and believed.

18 and arrested the apostles and put them under custody in the public jail.
19 But during the night an angel from the Lord opened the doors of the prison, led them out and said,
20 "Go, take your place on the temple grounds and speak to the people the message about this life."
21 So, on hearing this, they entered the temple grounds about daybreak and taught.

---

throughout the New Testament. Jesus had been delivered up out of envy, the Jews from Thessalonica persecuted Paul out of envy, and here, it also raises its ugly head. Jealousy will lead to persecution again and again. Warn counselees about the dire consequences of jealousy and envy. These leaders thought only of themselves, rather than rejoicing at the coming of a Savior, at the healing power of God released in their midst, and at the help their people were receiving. They thought, "They have stolen the hearts of the people from us." Jealousy is a highly self-centered emotion. And it can lead to murder. The desire is to get rid of the person envied. So they arrested the apostles once more, this time placing them in **the public jail** (v. 18).

But God would have nothing of it. He sent an **angel** to free them from **prison** (v. 19). The angel also gave them a message from God: "**Go, take your place on the temple grounds and speak to the people the message about this life.**" God told them to defy rulers who had overstepped their bounds as servants of the state. Without a doubt, there is a time to disobey; God Himself made this clear by the angel's command.[1] As the disciples said to the leaders of the nation, they would have to decide who should be obeyed—God or them (4:19). For them the answer was plain—they would obey God (cf. v. 29). Disobedience to authority should take place only on those rare occasions when a Christian is required to sin. God gave no one the right to order anyone to sin.

At **daybreak** they did as the angel commanded (v. 21). The rulers then discovered that they were gone (vv. 21-24). The guards didn't under-

---

[1] There are four separate authority-submission spheres in the New Testament: the home, the church, the state, the marketplace. But these are limited by Scriptural parameters. They do not overlap. Whenever someone gives orders that are beyond the bounds of authority granted to his sphere of activity, he is speaking on his own arrogated authority, not God's. Nothing in one sphere contradicts anything in another. No one is given power to order another to sin. Had the apostles obeyed the rulers, they would have sinned against God.

Now the high priest arrived, and those who were with him, and convened the meeting of the Sanhedrin and all the senate of the sons of Israel, and sent for them to be brought from the prison.

22 But when the officers got there, they couldn't find them in the jail, so they returned and reported, saying,

23   We found the prison securely shut and the guards standing at the doors, but when we opened them, we didn't find anyone inside.

24 Now when the captain of the temple and the chief priests heard these words, they were at a loss to understand them and wondered what all this might come to.

25 Then somebody came and told them, "Come see, the men that you put in prison are standing on the temple grounds, teaching the people."

26 Then the captain with the officers went and brought them, but not with force, because they were afraid that people might stone them.

27 Now when they brought them, they made them appear before the Sanhedrin. And the high priest questioned them, saying,

28   We gave you strict orders not to teach in this name, yet you've filled Jerusalem with your teaching! You plan to bring this man's blood on us.

29 Peter and the apostles said,
       We must obey God rather than men.

30   Our fathers' God raised Jesus, Whom you killed by hanging Him on a tree.

---

stand, the rulers were perplexed. God's ways often bring confusion and consternation to those who oppose them. Finally, they heard that the apostles were back on their soapbox in the temple again, just as if nothing had happened (v. 25)! Fearing the people's reaction, the guards brought them quietly to the rulers (v. 26). The High Priest questioned them, first accusing them of disobedience and of **bringing** Jesus' **blood on them**. As a matter of fact, they, themselves, were the ones who had taken Christ's **blood** (culpable guilt for taking His life) **upon** themselves (Matthew 27:25). Peter and the apostles were preaching nothing but the facts and their terrible implications for those who were responsible for the cross, but failed to repent.

Then came Peter's great statement, **"We must obey God rather than men"** (v. 29) which must rank along with his word recorded in 4:19, 20. The Spirit of God brought forth from his lips great declarations that all of us down through the ages ought to admire and emulate in our own ministries. It was a courageous statement that exhibited the boldness

31   God exalted this Man to a place at His right hand as a Ruler and
      Savior to give repentance and forgiveness of sins to Israel.

32   We are witnesses of these things, and so is the Holy Spirit that
      God gave to those who obey Him.

33 When they heard this, they were cut to the heart and intended to kill
them.

34 But a certain Pharisee in the Sanhedrin named Gamaliel, a teacher of
the law who was honored by all the people, stood up and ordered them to
put these men outside for a little while.

35 Then he said to them,
      Men of Israel, be careful about what you intend to do to these
      men.

36   Earlier, Theudas arose, claiming that he was somebody, and about
      four hundred men turned toward him, but when he was killed, all
      those who followed him were dispersed, and the movement came
      to nothing.

37   Later on Judas the Galilean came into prominence in the days of
      the census and drew away people after him. That man also per-
      ished, and all who followed him were scattered.

38   So, now I tell you, stay away from these men and let them alone.
      If this plan or this work is from men, it will fail,

39   but if it is from God, you won't be able to stop them, and you will
      find yourselves fighting God!

---

the Lord provided.

Once more Peter takes the opportunity to present the message to the
Sanhedrin (vv. 30-32). But, instead of repenting, they are further hardened
and **intended to kill** Peter. But God was at work even in the lives of this
corrupt body. There was one man, **Gamaliel**, who brought order and reason to the discussion (vv. 34-39). It is interesting how God works. Satan
isn't the only one who infiltrates enemy ranks. From time to time you will
receive help from unexpected quarters.

Gamaliel cautioned moderation. He mentioned previous events in
which matters seemed to get out of hand, but eventually came to naught
(vv. 36, 37). A very valid statement is made in verses 38 and 39. If the
movement is from men, it will fail; if it is from God, there is nothing to do
to curtail it anyway. But, in the process, a person might be found **fighting
God!** That would be truly serious. It would seem that either Gamaliel had
great wisdom or, in addition to that, he suspected that there might be
something to what the apostles were teaching. At any rate, he posits the
possibility that the apostles may be men from God.

40 So they followed his advice; and they called back the apostles, beat them, ordered them not to speak in Jesus' name and released them.

41 Then they left the presence of the Sanhedrin, rejoicing that they were considered worthy to be dishonored on behalf of the Name.

42 Every day in the temple, and from house to house, they regularly taught and preached the good news about Jesus as the Christ.

Peter's message got through. They were **cut to the heart** (v. 33), but not in repentance as opposed to the crowds who believed (2:37). The apostolic message penetrated the heart. It did not bounce off the exterior as so much of our preaching and counseling does. Perhaps the principal reason is because there was an extraordinary amount of boldness in their speech, and there is so little in ours. They were not afraid to "tell it like it is." We are. Our counselors tend to hedge when talking of sin. Peter, however, again and again came right out with words like this: **Our father's God raised up Jesus Whom you killed by hanging Him on a tree** (v. 30). When speaking of sin, we tend to fudge. But truly biblical counselors will be biblical to the extent that they are fearlessly frank. But in taking this matter-of-fact approach, they must also be careful never to be vindictive.

So, against all canons of justice, they beat **the apostles** and once more **ordered them not to speak in Jesus' name.** The apostles, beaten and bruised, **rejoiced that they were considered worthy to be dishonored on behalf of the Name** (v. 41). Would your counselee consider it an honor to be beaten and dishonored for the sake of Christ? When he is able to rejoice in suffering for Christ, rather than complaining, whining, getting angry about it, he probably has been successfully counseled.

Once more, the apostles disobeyed the orders given to them and **preached and taught regularly** (v. 42). It was not that they sneaked out into the crowd to teach whenever the rulers were not looking. No. They went to their normal place and could be counted on to appear on the scene every day regardless of who was there. Some counselees will obey in "safe" ways. The apostles obeyed God regardless of whether it was safe to do so or not. That is the spirit of obedience that you need to instill in counselees. Obedience to God is a major issue in counseling. It must never be conditional ("I'll obey God if. . ."). It must always be complete (no fudging allowed). It must be in strict accordance with God's Word (no alterations will do). And it must be immediate (no postponing to a more convenient time). You may wish to write this—or something comparable—on a card that can be handed to counselees to carry as a reminder.

CHAPTER 6

1 Now in these days, as there was a growing number of disciples, the Hellenists raised a complaint against the Hebrews, because their widows were being overlooked during the daily serving of food.
2   So the Twelve called a general meeting of the disciples and said,
    It isn't right for us to stop preaching God's Word to serve tables.

We encounter more trouble in this chapter. But the church was able to solve it with alacrity, and in God's providence, the diaconate was formed as an office in the church. There were **Hellenists** in the church (that is, Greek-speaking Jews from elsewhere who had recently become Christians). They thought that their widows were being neglected in favor of the Hebrew widows in the daily allocating of funds and food (v. 1). The complaint was reasonable, and if there was substance to it, (as it seems there was) something *should* have been done. The Hellenists did the right thing; instead of holding this in and becoming bitter, they went to the church. In response, the Twelve then also did the right thing. They chose seven solid men *with hellenistic names* to administer the alms (v. 5). The **entire body** concurred. The interesting fact is that a decision was made out of wisdom. That is the reason for having a body of people to make decisions—not everything can be thought through beforehand and laid out as a rule. You need wise people to help apply general principles to specific situations.

It is utterly important for counselors to instruct counselees to take their general grievances to the church authorities rather than gossip about them and become increasingly bitter and resentful. Many, instead, decide to leave, case divisions, or even get the law involved.[1] Always insist on settling matters, and settling them before the church in a proper manner (cf. Matthew 18:15ff.).

In the discussion of the widows some very important matters emerged. The apostles said that it wasn't right for them to take time away from the work to which they had been called in order to **serve tables**. It was not that the apostles thought it beneath them to wait on tables; that wasn't the problem. But it was wrong to curtail the preaching of the gospel and prayer for some other work (v. 2). They had been called by Christ

---

[1] But see I Corinthians 6 on going to court.

3   Now then, brothers, look for seven of your men who have a good reputation, full of the Spirit and wisdom, that we may appoint them to this work,

4   while we will continue to devote ourselves to prayer and the ministry of the Word.

5   This word seemed right to the entire body, so they chose Stephen, a man full of the Holy Spirit and faith, Philip, Prochorus, Nicanor, Timon, Parmenas and Nicolas, a proselyte from Antioch.

6   They had them stand before the apostles, and they prayed and laid their hands on them.

7 God's Word spread, and the number of the disciples increased greatly in Jerusalem, and a great many of the priests became obedient to the faith.

---

to a specific task and, as important as other tasks might be, they were to do what He had bid them do. That principle applies to counselees who are failing to do what they ought to do. Many times they spread themselves so thin over secondary issues that they aren't able to do any one thing well. Luke describes the apostles' work as the **ministry of the Word** (v. 4). The word **ministry** is akin to the word **serve** in verse 2.[1] A person who is preaching or counseling is serving also. But he serves the Word rather than tables! Counseling is the other half of the ministry of the Word. It is not a separate, unrelated activity as some, (who think it is applying the principles of psychology to counselees), seem to view it. Counseling is the use of Scripture to help believers grow by grace through solving problems God's way.

The congregation as a whole selected the men, but the apostles ordained them[2] (v. 3, 6). The qualifications for the office included having a **good reputation** (after all they were handling funds), being **Spirit filled** (to enable them to fulfil their various tasks) and having **wisdom** (this would be needed to meet further controversies that might arise). These are still the qualifications for a deacon. When you boil down the diaconal qualifications listed in I Timothy, they amount to the same thing. The fundamental principle behind the diaconal office, then, is this: to do whatever tasks the elders assign to them in order to relieve the elders from getting involved in activities that would hinder them from accomplishing their

---

[1] *diakonia*; the work of "deaconing."

[2] Ordination is not some magical act. It simply means to appoint (or set aside) to a task.

8 Now Stephen, full of grace and power, did great wonders and signs among the people.

9 Then some of those from the synagog of Freedmen (as it was called), and some of the Cyrenians, the Alexandrians and some from Cilicia rose up and disputed with Stephen.

10 But they couldn't stand up against the wisdom and the spirit with which he spoke.

11 Then they put some men up to saying, "We have heard him speak blasphemous words against Moses and God."

12 So they stirred up the people and the elders and the scribes, and they went after him and seized him and brought him before the Sanhedrin.

13 The false witnesses appeared and said,

> This man regularly speaks words against this holy place and the law.

---

tasks. Sometimes people have thought that deacons were merely to do eleemosynary works. But that is wrong. The matter that occasioned their appointment was of that nature, but the principle that brought the office into being was much larger. They should do *whatever tasks* the elders give them to do that would otherwise keep the elders from *their* assigned tasks. The deacons are, therefore, a very important catchall body.

Next, we are told about **Stephen**, one of the first deacons, who became the first martyr (actually, chapters 6, and most of 7, are of a piece[1]). There were Jews from a Greek-speaking synagog who disputed with Stephen[2] (v. 9), but they were unable to refute him (v. 10). So, since they couldn't win the debate, they decided to undermine the man by twisting his words. Accordingly, they accused him of speaking **blasphemous words against Moses and God** (v. 11). Of course Stephen had done nothing of the sort. But by these false accusations they **stirred up the people and the elders and the scribes** who seized Stephen and brought him before the Sanhedrin. When they actually appeared, the **false witnesses** said that Stephen spoke against the **temple** and the **law:** that Jesus would destroy the temple and change the old order of things introduced by **Moses**. There was just enough truth in these accusations to make them stick with those who had heard him speak. Doubtless Stephen had said *similar* things, but with an entirely different meaning and intent.[3] The

---

[1] It might have been more helpful to begin chapter 7 at 6:8.

[2] There were 480 synagogs in Jerusalem with all sorts of distinctions.

[3] It is not uncommon for unbelievers to misinterpret, then misuse your words.

14   The fact is that we have heard him say that this Jesus, the Naza-
        rene, will destroy this place and will change the customs that
        Moses delivered to us.

15 All who sat in the Sanhedrin stared at Stephen, because his face looked
like the face of an angel.

---

face of Stephen was as innocent as that of an **angel**; everyone has reason
to believe that he had been falsely accused. Yet that did not deter them
from opposing him and his message (v. 15). Possibly, jealousy was part of
the motivation in this case also (see chapter 5).

Is it news that people falsely accuse others when they can't refute
them? Certainly not. You will find this is a common occurrence among
those your counselees engage in discussion. They, in turn, ought to be told
to stick to their guns as Stephen did. People will twist their words either
because they do not understand (truth can only be appreciated fully by
believers as I Corinthians 2 indicates) or because they think that in the end
they must win the argument in some way—or both. Here, it seems that
both were true.

CHAPTER 7

1 Then the high priest said, "Are these things true?"

2 He said,

Brothers and fathers, listen to me. The God of glory appeared to our father Abraham when he was in Mesopotamia, before he lived in Haran,

3 and told him, **"Leave your land and your relatives and go to a land that I will show you."**

4 So he left the land of the Chaldeans and lived in Haran. After his father died, God moved him from there to the land in which you are now living;

5 but He didn't give him an inheritance in it—not even a piece of ground a foot long—but He promised **to give it to him and to his descendants as a possession, even though he didn't have a child.**

6 God told him this: **Your descendants will be aliens in a foreign land, where they will be enslaved and ill-treated for four hundred years.**

7 **Then I will judge the nation to which they are enslaved,** God said, **and after that they will leave it and worship Me in this place.**

I shall not attempt to consider the longest sermon in the book of Acts verse by verse. Rather, I shall simply summarize it and then make a few observations. The sermon is important because it occasioned the crisis which definitively separated Christianity from Judaism. Until then, the church was viewed as a sect of the Jews. Afterward, it would be considered that which it was—a separate religion.[1] Of course, the final separation, when the last vestiges of Jewish Christianity were dissolved, was at the destruction of Jerusalem and the temple in 70 AD.

Stephen was accused of undermining Moses' law and denying the permanent sanctity of the temple. His sermon is a reply to both charges. Stephen, in essence, said this: in God's economy both the law of Moses

---

[1] It was not that Christians set up a separate religion. It is actually what the Jews did when they rejected their own religion's teachings and prophecies about the Messiah. Judaism (even of an orthodox sort) is not the religion of the Old Testament.

8 He gave him the covenant of circumcision, and so he became Isaac's father and circumcised him on the eighth day. Isaac became the father of Jacob, and Jacob of the twelve patriarchs.

9 The patriarchs became jealous of Joseph and sold him into Egypt; but God was with him

10 and rescued him from all his afflictions and gave him grace and wisdom, so that he was recognized by Pharaoh, king of Egypt. And he appointed him governor over all of Egypt and all his household.

11 Then a famine came over all of Egypt and Canaan, and there was a lot of hardship, and our fathers couldn't find any food.

12 So when Jacob heard that there was wheat in Egypt, he sent our fathers for the first time.

13 But on the second trip Joseph made himself known to his brothers, and Joseph's family became known by Pharaoh.

14 Then Joseph sent and called for his father Jacob and all his relatives—seventy-five persons.

15 So Jacob went down to Egypt, and it was there that he and our fathers died.

16 Their remains were taken to Shechem and placed in the tomb that Abraham bought for a sum of money from Hamor's sons in Shechem.

17 As the time for God to fulfill the promise He had made to Abraham drew near, the people in Egypt greatly increased in number.

18 At length **a different Egyptian king arose who didn't know about Joseph**.

19 He took advantage of our race and mistreated our fathers by forcing them to expose their babies so that they would die.

20 Moses was born at this time, and was delightful in God's sight. For three months he was raised in his father's house,

21 but when he was exposed Pharaoh's daughter adopted him and raised him as her own son.

22 So Moses was trained in all the Egyptians' wisdom, and he spoke and acted with power.

23 Now when he was forty years old, it came into his heart to visit his brothers, the sons of Israel.

24 But when he saw one of them being injured, he defended him and avenged the one who was wronged by striking down the Egyptian.

25 Now he thought that his brothers would understand that God was going to rescue them by his hand, but they didn't understand this.

26 Then, the next day, Moses appeared on the scene where two Jews were fighting and tried to bring peace by reconciling them, saying, "Men, you're brothers! Why are you injuring each other?"

27   But the man who was injuring his neighbor thrust him aside, say-ing, "**Who appointed you a ruler over us?**

28   **You don't want to kill me like you killed the Egyptian yester-day, do you?**"

29   So **Moses fled at this word and became an exile in the land of Midian,** where he became the father of two sons.

   30   When forty years had passed, **an angel appeared to him in the flames of a burning thorn bush while he was in the desert near Mount Sinai,**

31   When Moses saw it, he was startled by the sight, and when he approached it to examine it more closely, the Lord's voice came:

32   "**I am the God of your fathers, the God of Abraham, Isaac and Jacob.**" Moses started to tremble and didn't dare look.

33   **Then the Lord said to him, "Loosen the sandals on your feet; the place where you are standing is holy ground.**

34   I **have seen the ill treatment of My people in Egypt, and I heard their groans, so I have come down to set them free. Come now, I will send you to Egypt.**"

   35   This **Moses**—the one whom they rejected, saying, "**Who appointed you a ruler and a judge?**"—God sent as a ruler and redeemer with the assistance of the angel who appeared to him in the bush.

36   This man led them out, performing wonders and signs in the land of Egypt, in the Red Sea and in the desert for forty years.

37   This is the Moses who told Israel's sons, "**From among your brothers God will raise up a Prophet like me.**"

38   This man is the one who was in the church in the desert together with the angel who spoke to him at Mount Sinai with our fathers, who received living oracles to give to us.

39   This is the one our fathers wouldn't obey, but thrust him aside and in their hearts turned back to Egypt,

40   **saying to Aaron, "Make gods for us who will lead us; we don't know what has happened to this Moses who led us out of the land of Egypt.**"

41   So at that time they made a calf and offered a sacrifice to the idol and applauded the works of their hands!

42   But God turned away and delivered them over to the worship of the stars of the sky, as it is written in the prophets' book,
      You didn't offer victims and sacrifices to Me forty years in the desert, did you, house of Israel?

43   **Indeed, you carried Moloch's tent**
      and the god Rephan's star,
      the images you made to worship—
      and I will deport you beyond Babylon.

44 Our fathers had the testimony tent in the desert, just as the One Who spoke to Moses commanded him according to the model that he had seen.

45 Our fathers received it and brought it in with Joshua when they took possession of the nations that God drove out from the presence of our fathers until David's time.

46 He found favor with God and prayed that he might find a dwelling for Jacob's God.[1]

47 But Solomon built a house for Him.

48 However, the Most High doesn't dwell in places made by hands (as the prophet says):

49 **Heaven is My throne and earth is a stool for My feet. What sort of house will you build for Me, says the Lord, or in what place will I rest?**

50 **Didn't My hand make all these things?**

51 You stiffnecked people, uncircumcised in hearts and ears! You always resist the Holy Spirit. As your fathers did, so do you!

---

[1] Some MSS read, *for Jacob's house.*

---

and the temple had served their purposes. Because of that, they had to give way to a more spiritual way of worship (cf. John 4:24). This new way was in continuity with the old. It was what Mosaic laws typified. The new was the reality of which the old was but the shadow.

There are three lines of thought, sometimes intertwined and sometimes separated in Stephen's message. First, he showed from the history of the people that the original covenant was given not to Moses, but to Abraham. This was a spiritual covenant. It had few of the material aspects of Mosaic ritual. If it was acceptable *before* Moses, why could it not be afterwards? Second, Stephen pointed out that God was worshipped acceptably *before* there was a tabernacle or a temple. Why could He not be worshipped that way afterwards? After all, this history reveals that God's dealings with His people were not uniform in every area. Third, Stephen warned the Sanhedrin that they had become like the fathers who persecuted the prophets. They were part of a tradition that consistently opposed God down through the years. As the fathers did, so had they done; except that it was not a mere prophet they persecuted, it was their Messiah Whom they murdered!

Up until verse 51, they heard him out: but when Stephen turned the light of the discourse on them, exposing their sin, they were **pierced**

49

52	Which of the prophets didn't your fathers persecute? And they killed those who predicted the coming of the Righteous One, of Whom you now have become the murderers and betrayers—
53	you, who received the law at the order of angels—and didn't keep it!

54 Now when they heard these things, they were pierced through to their hearts and gnashed their teeth at him.

55 But he, full of the Holy Spirit, gazed at the sky and saw God's glory and Jesus standing at God's right hand, and said,

56 "There, I see the heavens opened up, and the Son of Man standing at God's right hand!"

57 Then they shouted with a loud voice and covered their ears and rushed on him with one thought in mind.

58 They threw him out of the city and stoned him. And the witnesses took off their clothes and laid them at the feet of a young man named Saul.

---

through to their hearts and gnashed their teeth at him (v. 54). His message got through, but there was no repentance—only fury. When truth penetrates hearts, they either melt in repentance or harden in rage.

How was Stephen able to communicate so much before he was stopped? He used the inductive method: like the beasts in Revelation, the stinger was in the tail of his message. He moved from particular to particular, pasting together a historical picture that led to his conclusion. It was only after he had them squarely within the net, that he pulled the string and caught them dangling! Whenever you are dealing with a hostile person or persons in counseling, it is well to employ this method. Move from the specific to the general; from facts to a conclusion. When dealing with those who are friendly to you and your message, go the other way—reason deductively. In the deductive method, you move from the conclusion (the general) to the supporting evidence (the particulars). In that way you can emphasize your conclusion over and over, until it is indelibly imprinted upon the mind.

Angry as they were, because, like Peter, Stephen had exposed their sin, what he said after the speech infuriated them even more. Looking toward the sky, Stephen saw the glory cloud of God with Jesus standing at the right hand of it (v. 55). He had the temerity to say so. When his words placed Jesus at the Father's right hand, that was the straw that broke the camel's back for them. They rushed on him, drove him out of the city, and stoned him. It should have been the point at which they fell to their knees and acknowledged Jesus as the Messiah Whom the Lord had set on His

59 As they were stoning Stephen, he prayed, saying, "Lord Jesus, receive my spirit."
60 Then he knelt down and shouted with a loud voice, "Lord, don't hold this sin against them!" And when he had said this, he fell asleep.

---

throne. Daniel's prophecy in chapters 2 and 7 and Psalm 2 had been fulfilled. It was time for humility and rejoicing.

But in the midst of the stoning, as he was dying, Stephen asked God to receive his spirit and prayed **"Lord don't hold this sin against them."** That is the prayer that counselees ought to be able to pray when they are done in by an enemy. However, seldom is Stephen's attitude found among those who seek counsel. If it were, fewer would find it necessary to come for counseling in the first place. Instead, as a rule, what you encounter is one of two responses: either a "poor me" attitude, in which the whiner seeks pity and sympathy, or vindictive anger ("I'll get him for that!"). It will be your task to move the counselee from either of the latter two to the former. You may use this text profitably to do so along with Jesus' words from the cross, "Father forgive them" (Luke 23:34).

The people who stoned Stephen laid their clothes at the feet of Saul (who was to become the apostle Paul), a young man who was there looking on. Many have thought that Paul was so impressed that he never forgot the substance of Stephen's message and that, after his conversion, he structured his messages and letters, at least in part, after it.[1]

The text says that Stephen's **face** looked like that of an **angel** (6:15). Perhaps this refers to a certain glow about it or, as I suggested earlier, perhaps it was the honesty and innocence of his face that are in view. However, to these men, it made no difference. Had a genuine angel given this speech, they would have tried to stone him. After all, they murdered Jesus Christ!

---

[1] On this point compare verse 48 with 17:24; verse 53 with Galatians 3:19; verse 51 with Romans 2:28; verse 60 with II Timothy 4:16; verses 5-8 with Romans 4:10-19. Ker, in his *History of Preaching*, says that Paul's sermon at Antioch follows Stephen's pattern.

CHAPTER 8

1 Now Saul was in complete agreement with killing him.
And on that day a great persecution broke out against the church at Jerusalem, and everybody was scattered throughout the regions of Judea and Samaria except the apostles.
2   Devout men buried Stephen and loudly mourned over him.
3   But Saul ravaged the church; entering house after house, he dragged out men and women and imprisoned them.

Continuing the narrative that carries over into this chapter from the last, we read that Saul (later to become the apostle Paul) was **in complete agreement with killing** Stephen. As a matter of fact, it seems that he was motivated by it to do all that he could to stamp out the new Christian heresy. We read that, like a dog that has gotten a taste of blood, **he ravaged the church,** and **entering house after house, he dragged out men and women and imprisoned them** (v. 3). The **great persecution against the church at Jerusalem** that **broke out that day** was, it seems, headed up by Saul.

When you see in someone excessive zeal for something, you know that there is a possibility of seeing an "about face" in him. And, of course, that is precisely what happened (chapter 9). Jesus once said to one of the churches in Revelation that He would rather have them cold or hot; but not lukewarm (3:16)! When a counselee protests strongly about something,[1] you know that there is a possibility that he will at length come over to a biblical viewpoint. How is that? Well, the lukewarm person is apathetic; those who are hot or cold are *concerned*. Concern keeps one thinking (often, even studying) about the opposition and their beliefs. There was no apathy in Saul.

Because of the persecution, which from this point on was a regular way in which the church was scattered so as to spread the message, God sowed the gospel seed throughout the Mediterranean world.[2] Until this juncture, the church had been bottled up in Jerusalem. Now it was beginning to follow the divine pattern laid out in Acts 1:8 by the Lord Jesus.

---

[1] Genuinely; not in some hypocritical display.

[2] Providentially, Saul may have done as much to spread the gospel before as after conversion.

4 As a result, those who were scattered abroad went everywhere announcing the message of good news.

5   Philip, for instance, went down to a city of Samaria and preached Christ to them.

6   The crowds unitedly paid attention to the things Philip said when they heard and saw the signs he was performing.

7   Unclean spirits, shouting with a loud voice, came out of many of those who had been possessed by them, and many paralytics and lame persons were healed.

8   So there was much joy in that city.

9 Now a certain man, named Simon, had been practicing magic in the city for some time, and had astounded the nation of Samaria. He claimed that he was somebody great,

---

Verses 1 and 4 need to be compared. Notice, all *except* **the apostles** were **scattered**. And then notice that **those who were scattered abroad went everywhere announcing the message of good news**. There are overly zealous Christians who think that only the ordained officials of the church ought to evangelize. That, evidently, was not what God thought; He drove out the church (all *except* the officers) and they—the common, ordinary, everyday believers—went everywhere spreading the good news. God's plan was for *everyone* to *evangelize everywhere*. Keep that in mind. Your counselee may have any number of opportunities to evangelize that he is not entering into. Help direct him. Some of those opportunities may have opened up through some persecution aimed at him (probably nothing of the magnitude that was occurring here in Jerusalem). We must all be alert to see how trial and difficulty bring about opportunities. Counselees, focused on self and their experiences, are not likely to be attuned to these opportunities. You are probably the one to point them out. Indeed, when one focuses on opportunities, he has learned to look outside of himself and, usually as a result, finds it easier to bear up under trial. Self-centeredness, the rage of our age, is quite destructive of Christian growth and service. The church has not been helped by those who have spread self-image teaching abroad in the name of Christ when it was nothing more than a pagan view.

We next read about the work of **Philip**, another of the deacons. In the scattering, he went down to **Samaria** and **preached Christ** (v. 5). The preaching effort was highly successful (vv. 6-8). But again there arose a problem. **Simon**, who **had been practicing magic**, and **claimed that he was somebody great**, also claimed to believe the gospel (whether v. 13

10   and they all—from the smallest to the greatest—paid attention to him, saying, "This man is the one who is called the Great Power of God."
11   They all paid attention to him, because for a considerable time he had astounded them by his magic.
12   But when they believed Philip's preaching about God's empire and the name of Jesus Christ, they were baptized, both men and women.
13   Even Simon himself believed, and when he was baptized, he attached himself to Philip, and as he saw the signs and great miracles taking place, he was astounded.
14   Now when the apostles in Jerusalem heard that Samaria had accepted God's word, they sent Peter and John to them.
15   They went down and prayed for them, so that they might receive the Holy Spirit
16   (so far, He hadn't fallen on any of them; they had simply been baptized in the name of the Lord Jesus).
17   Then they laid their hands on them and they received the Holy Spirit.
18   But when Simon saw that the Spirit was given by the laying on of the apostles' hands, he offered them money, saying,

---

means that he believed savingly or not is difficult to say). It seems that he was fascinated by the **signs and great miracles** that **were taking place**. Presumably, what Philip was doing so outclassed Simon that the people began flocking to Philip instead of Simon. Along with the others who professed faith, Simon was baptized into church fellowship. The apostles heard about what was happening in Samaria and they sent Peter and John to them, who prayed for the Samaritan believers to receive the Holy Spirit. When they laid their hands on them the Spirit was given.[1] It is interesting to note that there are only two instances of the Spirit having been given directly: Pentecost and at the first coming of the Spirit among the Gentiles (Acts 10). The two other instances, one of which follows each of the direct gifts, are this one and in Acts 19 at Ephesus. In those cases, the Spirit came by the imposition of apostolic hands. Evidently, after Peter exercised his right of opening the door of the church to the Jews and to the Gentiles (the use of the keys; cf. Matthew 16:18ff.), there were no more such unmeditated outpourings of the Spirit. That is an important point to raise with counselees who are earnestly waiting for the Spirit to descend on them. They will wait endlessly for something that simply isn't going to take place!

---

[1] Laying on of hands is the visible sign of granting a gift or office to someone.

19 "Give me this authority too, so that whoever I lay hands on may receive the Holy Spirit."
20 But Peter said to him,
   Your silver perish with you for thinking that God's gift could be bought with money!
21   You have no part or share in the proclamation of this message, because your heart isn't right before God.
22   Therefore, repent of this wickedness of yours and pray to the Lord, so that perhaps He will forgive the intention of your heart.

Simon's story is continued in verses 18 through 24: **When Simon saw that the Spirit was given by the laying on of the apostles' hands he offered them money, saying, "Give me this authority too."** Peter was incensed at this crass action. He declared that Simon and his money would perish for thinking that he could buy the gift of God.[1] Then, he made this trenchant statement, **"You have no part or share in the proclamation of this message, because your heart isn't right before God"** (v. 21). Counselor, the same applies to you. God doesn't need numbers of people ministering in His Name. He wants only those whose hearts are right toward Himself. No one else has a right to "minister" in His Name. There are already too many who call themselves "Christian counselors" whose counseling isn't Christian in content, method, or orientation. If those who are a part of the eclectic scene were to seek to become a part of the biblical counseling movement because they saw such better results, they would not be welcome unless their hearts were right before God. If they were fit to minister, however, they would be welcomed with open arms into the movement. But the matter of their relationship toward God and His Word is uppermost. They cannot adopt biblical techniques *per se*, and forget that the power behind those techniques is the Lord Himself. Without His power, all is a sham. At every level, Christianity is a matter of one's relationship to Christ. Peter called on Simon to **repent** and **pray** that Jesus would **forgive** the **intention** of his **heart**. His heart wasn't right because his *intention* was not to do the Lord's work, but to gain greater fame by working Spirit-powered miracles. It is possible for counselors to counsel with similar intentions. Have you checked *your* heart lately?

When Peter said that Simon was in **the gall of bitterness and bond of unrighteousness** it seems, as F.F. Bruce intimates, that he was still

---

[1] The word "simony" today is used to describe the purchase of ecclesiastical power or office.

23   I see you are in the gall of bitterness and bond of unrighteousness. 24 Then Simon replied, "You pray to the Lord for me, so that the things you have said won't happen to me."

   25 So then, when they had borne witness to and spoken the Lord's word, they returned to Jerusalem, preaching the good news in many of the Samaritan villages.

   26 Now an angel from the Lord spoke to Philip and said, "Get up and go south along the road that leads from Jerusalem to Gaza." (This is a desert road.)

---

unregenerate. And even when he asked Peter to pray for him, Bruce thinks that he asked out of his fear of men (men with the power that Peter and John possessed).

The self-centered technique mongering that we see in Simon is not confined to him or to would-be counselors alone. There are counselees who want change in their lives in order to achieve some selfish end. All such counselees must be told plainly that the change God effects is change that grows out of the *intention* to develop a right relationship to Him. They must be led away from thinking about techniques into thinking that seeks to honor Christ and make their lives a blessing to others. They must see that change in the counseling session and throughout the week comes not from following precepts or practices primarily, but from a growing willingness to believe and obey Christ. They must be helped to see that counseling is fundamentally between them and the Lord; and that like Peter and John, the counselor is but one who assists them to deal properly with Him. At bottom counseling is relational; not merely mechanical—following a set of roles or using certain techniques.

The apostles returned to Jerusalem. But God had other work for Philip to do. An **angel spoke to Philip** telling him to go to the coastal road from Jerusalem to Gaza. He obeyed, in spite of the fact that under his ministry in Samaria there was a revival going on, there were young Christians to nurture, and there was a new church to organize. God's ways are not always our ways. Opportunities and needs are not always the prime factor in determining where to minister. Counselees seeking wisdom about choices for their future must recognize that. Sometimes they are bowled over by opportunity and need (of course, these are factors to consider) and can see nothing else[1].

Philip was then introduced to the **Ethiopian eunuch** who was read-

---

[1] Such as unfulfilled responsibilities.

27 So he got up and went. And there he saw an Ethiopian, a eunuch, who was an official in charge of the entire treasury of Candace, queen of the Ethiopians. He had come to Jerusalem to worship,

28 and now as he was returning and sitting in his chariot, he was reading the prophet Isaiah.

29 The Spirit said to Philip, "Go and join him in the chariot."

30 So Philip ran up and heard him reading Isaiah the prophet and said, "Do you have any understanding of what you are reading?"

31 He said, "How could I, unless somebody guides me?" And he invited Philip to come up and sit with him.

32 Now the passage of Scripture that he was reading was this:

> **As a sheep He was led to the slaughter,**
> **and as a lamb before those who shear it is quiet,**
> **so He doesn't open His mouth.**

33 > **In His humiliation justice was denied Him.**
> **Who can tell about His descendants,**
> **since His life is taken from the earth?**

34 Then the eunuch said to Philip, "About whom, I ask you, does the prophet say this—about himself or about somebody else?"

35 Then Philip opened his mouth, and beginning with this Scripture he announced the good news about Jesus to him.

36 As they went along the road, they came to some water, and the eunuch said, "Look, water; why can't I be baptized?"

---

ing Isaiah 53 as he returned home to Ethiopia.[1] Yes, Philip left great evangelistic opportunities to talk to one person—but that single person probably would be the one to introduce Christ to an entire nation! God's providence often diverges from our ideas about what to do. We must be willing to obey God's Word even when it doesn't make sense to us. Faith believes that God always makes sense—even when we don't understand how.

The eunuch was very honest about the fact that he didn't comprehend what he was reading (v. 31). Philip explained that the passage (Isaiah 53) referred to Jesus Christ (v. 35). Then, along that desert road, he **baptized** the eunuch into membership in Christ's church (v. 38). The average counselee doesn't understand many of the passages of the Bible that you will want to use in counseling. You must be able to explain them to him whenever he asks about them. You must also explain passages to

---

[1] Possibly referring here to the Sudan.

37 [1]

38 Then he ordered the chariot to stop, and they both went down to the water, both Philip and the eunuch, and he baptized him.

39 Then, when they came up out of the water, the Spirit of the Lord snatched Philip away, and the eunuch didn't see him any more, but he went his way rejoicing.

40 Now Philip was found in Azotus, and as he passed through he announced the good news to all the cities there until he reached Caesarea.

---

[1] Some MSS add vs. 37: *And Philip said, "If you believe with your whole heart you can." And he replied, "I believe that Jesus Christ is God's Son."*

---

them when they don't ask. Never use a passage of the Bible that you cannot interpret to someone else. Too often passages are simply thrown out to counselees as though the counselor expects them to understand them. Often they do not. If they don't, then one of two things may happen. Either they will misinterpret them (and subsequently use them for the wrong purposes, actually causing harm), or they will dismiss them as irrelevant. Either way the verses fail to help those who need them. While God can do anything He cares to do by means of His Word,[1] He nevertheless puts no premium on ignorance.

Having completed his task, the Spirit **snatched Philip away** and he was found next in **Azotus**, a town 20 miles North of Gaza. Then he went toward Caesarea, proclaiming the gospel in city after city along the way (v. 40). It is interesting that we see Philip here, there, and everywhere evangelizing. Philip is the closest thing to what today we would call a traveling evangelist (cf. Acts 21:8). And he was obedient!

---

[1] Even using it under such unfavorable conditions.

CHAPTER 9

1 But Saul, still breathing threats and murder against the Lord's disciples, went to the high priest
2 and asked him for letters to the synagogs at Damascus, so that if he found any who belonged to the Way, he might bind and bring them to Jerusalem.
3 On his trip he was drawing near to Damascus, when suddenly a light from the sky flashed around him.
4 Falling to the ground, he heard a voice saying to him,
  Saul, Saul, why are you persecuting Me?
5 He said, "Who are You, Lord?" And He said,
  I am Jesus, Whom you are persecuting.

In this chapter we read about the conversion of the apostle Paul. It begins with Saul **breathing threats and murder against the Lord's disciples** (v. 1). The intensity of the language mirrors the vehemence with which Saul lashed out against the infant church. As a dedicated Pharisee Saul was determined to stamp it out.[1] He, himself, had *initiated* the Damascus trip to attempt to apprehend any Christians who had fled Jerusalem in order to keep the new faith from spreading any farther (Saul *asked* **for letters to synagogs at Damascus**). He was dedicated to what he was doing. His being stopped in his tracks, turning about, and then beginning to preach the faith he formerly hated, took nothing less than a direct act of God.

A brilliant **light** shone from the **sky** and a **voice** asked, "**Saul, Saul, why are you persecuting Me?**" These words are important: Jesus counts those who persecute His disciples as persecuting Him. It is a serious thing to attack Christians. Counselees should be warned about attempting to do anything against other believers who may differ with them lest, in the end, they might be found persecuting (opposing, or insulting) Jesus.

Dumbfounded, having fallen to the ground, Saul asked, "**Who are You, Lord?**" His use of the expression **Lord** indicates that he recognized—or strongly suspected—that this was a divine intervention. In a day in which there was no technology for creating such a blaze of light or of amplifying and directing sound, what else was he to think? And he was

---

[1] See comments in the previous chapter about the conversion of those who are hot or cold.

6   Now, get up and go into the city, and you will be told what you
     must do.
   7 The men who were traveling with him stood speechless, hearing the
sound of a voice, but seeing nobody.
8   Saul got up from the ground, but when he opened his eyes he couldn't
see. So they led him by the hand and brought him into Damascus.
9   For three days he couldn't see and didn't eat or drink.

---

right. *Jesus* so clearly identified Himself to Saul that in his (Paul's) epistles written many years afterwards, he could speak with absolute certainty
about meeting the risen Lord. He too was a witness to the resurrection, as
an apostle had to be. No direct, divine intervention will bring people to
Christ today because the time of miracles is over and no one is becoming
an apostle; but all one needs to find Christ is the witness of the apostles
divinely recorded in the Bible. Providential events that stop people in their
tracks today may often be the prelude to radical change and commitment
to ministry. Counselors may be used in such circumstances to direct counselees to the change.

Jesus then told Saul to rise and go into the city where he would
receive directions as to what he must do. Those who were in the group
traveling with Saul were **speechless**. They saw the light, heard the sound
of the voice, but saw no one. That would be enough to render most of us
speechless—even today when there *is* technology by which to fake a comparable event (vv. 6, 7). Saul arose, temporarily blinded, and had to be **led**
into **Damascus**. For three days the Lord left him helpless, giving him time
to think. There are times when counselees do not need immediate help;
they are not ready to receive it. Rather, what they need is time to contemplate something or other that has happened. Instead of immediately telling
them what to do, because they may not have yet had time for events to
sink in, you should send them home to think. Being a Pharisee, Saul must
have done a great deal of rethinking about the Scriptures which he knew
so well, but had never understood properly. Your counselee may not know
the Bible as well as Saul did. You may have to send him home with particular Scriptures to think about.

During those sightless days, Saul neither ate nor drank anything, so
struck was he by what had happened to him (v. 9). It is almost inevitable
that a suddenly sightless person will be caught up in his thoughts. There
are times when matters so overshadow everything else, that food and
drink are the least of one's interests. When you meet a counselee who has
been going without such necessities, you can be certain that (from his per-

10 Now at Damascus there was a certain disciple named Ananias. The Lord said to him in a vision, "Ananias." He said, "Here I am, Lord."

11 The Lord said to him,

> Get up and go to the street called Straight, and in Judas' house ask for a man from Tarsus named Saul. He is praying,

12 > and he has had a vision of a man named Ananias coming in and putting his hands on him to enable him to see again.

13 But Ananias replied, "Lord, I have heard from a number of people about this man—how he has done many evil things to your saints at Jerusalem,

14 and that he has authority from the chief priests here to bind all those who call on Your name."

15 But the Lord said to him,

> Go, this man is My chosen vessel to carry My name before the Gentiles and kings and sons of Israel.

16 > I will show him how much he must suffer for My name's sake.

---

spective at least) something overwhelming has occurred.

Already in the city, God had alerted Ananias about Saul's coming (vv. 10ff.). He was directed to a certain house where Saul was **praying**. Thought had led to prayer. Having taken time to contemplate, rethink and pray Saul was now ready to hear what the Lord had for him. Ananias was directed to **lay hands on** Saul so that he might see once again (v. 12). Ananias meekly protested, having heard about Saul's violent opposition to the church (vv. 13, 14). How often Christians think they know better than God! Again and again in counseling, after already having clearly set forth what the Bible says, you will hear objections from counselees who, because of some information that they possess, think they know better than the Lord!. How foolish! He knows *all*. The best way to handle such objections is to insist on what the Bible says. In dealing with Ananias, God insisted that he obey.

God told Ananias that He had **chosen** Saul as a **vessel** in which to **carry His Name before the Gentiles, before kings, and before Israel,** and that **he must suffer much for His Name's sake** (vv. 15, 16). Doubtless Ananias eventually repeated this word from God to Saul. It was no secret, then, that he would undergo much suffering for Christ in days ahead. God's call realistically stated that suffering lay ahead. From the outset Saul knew what would be involved in ministry. It is important to be realistic with counselees. For instance, if you send someone back to his boss to confess that he stole money and try to make it right, you should

17 So Ananias left and entered the house. Then, laying his hands on him, he said,

> Brother Saul, the Lord Jesus, Who appeared to you on the road by which you came, has sent me to help you see again and be filled with the Holy Spirit.

18 At once something like scales fell from his eyes, and he saw again. Then, he got up and was baptized.

19 He ate some food and regained his strength. And for several days he was with the disciples in Damascus.

20 Now right away he began to preach in the synagogs that Jesus is God's Son.

---

tell him that he may have to suffer dire consequences. That, of course, is suffering of one's own making. On the contrary, there are many situations in which counselees by doing the right thing from the outset will bring down the wrath of unbelievers on them, just as Paul did when preaching the gospel. They must be alerted to the fact; otherwise, they may buckle under surprise at the response.

So Ananias obeyed. In laying his hands on Saul, he called him **brother**, recounted the event on the road to Damascus, and said that Jesus had instructed him to give him sight again and help him to be baptized with the Holy Spirit (v. 17). At once Saul could see and, to visibly confirm his Spirit baptism and membership in the church, was **baptized** with water (v. 18). Then he ate and remained for several days with the brothers in Damascus. Immediately there was a new camaraderie established. Concern for becoming one with the church and entering into its fellowship is a dominant theme the book of Acts. There were no lone wolf Christians. They all were added to the church immediately upon conversion. Many today claim to be Christians but remain outside the church. They cannot be *considered* such, even if they are in fact. They treat themselves as heathen and publicans. Aloofness is an unbiblical stance. When you encounter it in counseling, make it clear that it is sin not to come under the care and discipline of some congregation. Help counselees to make the right decision about which church to unite with. There are many who only vaguely know about liberalism and the differences between thoroughly Scriptural churches and those that are not. Counselors must be well informed—and inform others.

Saul had been a rabbi who had previously taught in synagogs. Then, right after his conversion he began to **preach Christ** in the **synagogs** of Damascus where there were many Jews. This caused quite a sensation

21 And everybody who heard was amazed and said,
> Isn't this the man who in Jerusalem devastated those who called on this Name? And hasn't he come here intending to bring them bound to the chief priests?

22 But Saul more and more was filled with power and confounded the Jews living in Damascus, proving that He is the Christ.

23 Now when many days had passed, the Jews plotted together to kill him, but Saul discovered their plot.

24 They carefully watched the gates day and night in order to kill him.

25 But at night his disciples took him and let him down through the wall in a basket.

26 When he returned to Jerusalem, he tried to join the disciples, but everybody was afraid of him; they didn't believe he was a disciple.

---

because the people had heard about Saul's fierce opposition to Christianity (vv. 20, 21). Saul was working hard at understanding his new faith and applying that understanding to his preaching. As he did, he was more and more **filled** with **power** and **confounded** the **Jews** (v. 22). When a new convert comes to Christ, if he uses the knowledge that he has to witness to his friends **right away** (every convert knows enough to lead another to Christ or he, himself, would not be saved) he will grow in his ability and effectiveness. Encourage new Christians to begin telling others about Christ as soon as possible.

Evidently, there were others who were nearly as zealous to destroy Christianity as Saul had been, so they hatched a **plot** to kill Saul. Somehow or other, he heard about this plan. He knew that they were **watching** the **gates** where they had decided to apprehend him. So, at night, the disciples let him down **over the wall** of the city in a large **basket**. It is not always right to meet the opposition head on—especially when minds are made up and people are bent on mayhem. It is often wise to go over the wall instead. Humiliating as it may have been, this expedient preserved Saul for great work in the days to come. Some counselees blunder into trouble that they don't need to face, often destroying their effectiveness for Christ. Teach them that under circumstances akin to Saul's, the better part of wisdom may be to escape.

So Saul returned to **Jerusalem**. Naturally he sought to affiliate with the church there, but the disciples were wary of him, thinking (probably) that this was some new ploy of his to discover and imprison more Christians (v. 26). But **Barnabas**, who was an encourager, stood up for Saul, recounted to the church what had happened on the road to and in the city

27 But Barnabas got hold of him and led him to the apostles, and told them how he saw the Lord on the road, and that He spoke to him, and how in Damascus he preached boldly in Jesus' name.

28 So he was with them in Jerusalem, going in and out, preaching boldly in the Lord's name.

29 He spoke and held disputations with the Hellenists, and they attempted to kill him.

30 But when the brothers learned about this, they brought him down to Caesarea and sent him off to Tarsus.

31 So then, the church throughout all Judea and Galilee and Samaria had peace and was built up; and by walking in the fear of the Lord and in the counsel of the Holy Spirit, it was enlarged.

32 Now in the course of Peter's travels throughout the area, he visited the saints living at Lydda.

33 There he found a certain man named Aeneas, who had been bedridden for eight years with a paralysis.

34 Peter said to him, "Aeneas, Jesus Christ is healing you. Get up and make your bed." And he got up at once.

35 All those who lived at Lydda and Sharon saw him, and they turned to the Lord.

36 Now in Joppa there was a certain disciple named Tabitha (which means "Dorcas," or "gazelle"). She was full of good works and acts of charity.

37 At that very time she happened to get sick and die; and when they had washed her they laid her in an upper room.

---

of **Damascus**, and vouched for him. The disciples received him and, not to get rid of him but to save him, personally helped him (probably at some financial expense) escape from Palestine through the port of **Caesarea** to his home town of **Tarsus** (v. 30). The section concludes with a progress report about how peace came to the church in Palestine and how it was built up (v. 31). Here is where the chapter should have ended. The rest of chapter 9 is a prelude to what follows in chapter 10.

Meanwhile at Lydda, as the result of another healing, Peter had an opportunity to preach the gospel, and many people from Lydda and the neighboring town of Sharon **turned to the Lord** (vv. 32-35). It is interesting that in the healing, once more, Peter is careful to give the credit to Jesus Christ (v. 34). How important for counselors not to glory in what they are able to do. Of course they do the counseling, just as Peter did the healing, but they have no more to offer people than Peter did in and of himself. Anything that happens that is beneficial to a counselee is from

38 Since Lydda was close to Joppa, when the disciples heard that Peter was there, they sent two men to urge him, "Don't hesitate; come to us!"

39 So Peter got up and went with them. When they arrived they led him up into the upper room, and all the widows stood by him, weeping and showing tunics and clothes that Dorcas made when she was with them.

40 Peter put them all outside and knelt down and prayed. Then, turning to the body, he said, "Tabitha, get up." And she opened her eyes, and when she saw Peter she sat up.

41 He gave her a hand and raised her up. Then he called the saints and the widows and presented her alive.

42 It became known throughout all Joppa, and many believed on the Lord.

43 Then he stayed in Joppa for a number of days with a tanner by the name of Simon.

Christ, not from the counselor who merely ministers it through His Word.[1]

In Joppa, Peter raised **Tabitha** (Dorcas) from the dead (vv. 36-43). The word got around and **many believed on the Lord**. Evidently, Tabitha had been a very useful person in the congregation and her death was a great loss. Church members sought out Peter to see if he could do anything about the problem. In God's providence, this matter brought him to Joppa. But God also had another reason for bringing him there. At Joppa, as we learn in the next chapter, Peter would use the keys that Jesus gave him again (Matthew 16:16ff.). There, he would unlock the door of the church to the Gentiles.

---

[1] Remember in chapter 6 how the apostles called themselves servants (ministers) of the Word. They were but waiters (deacons) of a different kind! The word *diaconos* has been translated in the Loeb Classical Library as "Lackey." It is not an office of honor, but of labor.

CHAPTER 10

1 Now there was a certain man in Caesarea named Cornelius, who was a centurion and belonged to what was called the Italian Cohort.

2 He was a devout man who feared God, together with all his household, and he gave liberally to people in need and regularly prayed to God.

3 About three o'clock in the afternoon he saw an unmistakable vision of an angel from God coming in and saying to him, "Cornelius."

4 He stared at him in terror and said, "What is it, Lord?" And he replied, Your prayers and your charity have ascended as a memorial before God.

5 Now, send men to Joppa and bring back Simon, who is called Peter.

6 He is staying with Simon the tanner, whose house is by the sea.

7 When the angel who had spoken to him left, he called two of his servants and a devout soldier who was one of those who assisted him,

8 explained everything to them and sent them off to Joppa.

At the beginning of chapter ten we meet **Cornelius**. Cornelius was a Roman **centurion** who was a **devout man** (though not a Hebrew) and who believed in the true God and supported good causes in connection with Judaism (vv. 1, 2). One afternoon, **about three o'clock an angel** appeared to him in a **vision**. He listened in **terror** while the angel told him that God had accepted his **prayers and charity.** The angel then instructed him to **send men to Joppa and bring Peter** from **Simon's house to Caesarea.** Cornelius explained what had happened to a believing soldier and some servants who attended him and sent them to get Peter (vv. 1-8). It is interesting to note that Cornelius had surrounded himself with fellow believers. As often as it is possible and legal to do so, it is well for Christians to do the same. Then they can operate best with others who understand why they do what they do. Sometimes counselees unnecessarily get into trouble with their faith because they have linked themselves with unbelievers whose values and practices are quite different. Good advice from a counselor will direct them accordingly.

In this regard there has been too much fraternization of Christians with Mormons and Roman Catholics. Much of this began with the misdirected ideas of those who thought of us as "co-belligerents" with them in fighting abortion and other issues as if we truly agreed. Political linking of this type can only lead to religious linking since all one does (even in politics) is religious. We should avoid wrong sorts of fraternization (II Corin-

9 Now the next day, about noon, as their travels brought them close to the city, Peter went up onto the roof to pray.

10 He grew hungry and wanted something to eat. But while they were preparing a meal, he went into a trance.

11 He saw the sky opened, and a sort of container like a huge sheet was being let down onto the earth by its four corners.

12 In it were all kinds of animals, and reptiles and birds of the sky.

13 A voice spoke to him, "Get up, Peter; kill and eat them."

14 But Peter said, "Oh no, Lord! I haven't ever eaten anything common and unclean."

15 Then the voice spoke to him a second time, "Don't treat as unclean what God has cleansed."

---

thians 6:14-18). As Cornelius' men were approaching Joppa **the next day about noon,** Peter went up to the **roof** of Simon's house to **pray.**[1] **In time, Peter grew hungry. While his host was preparing a meal,** Peter went into a **trance.** The word **trance** means that he was in a state in which he saw a vision. This vision from God that appeared in the opened sky was like a great container suspended by its four corners. **In it were all kinds of animals**—clean and unclean (vv. 11, 12). A heavenly voice told Peter to kill and eat them.[2] Peter objected, saying that he had never eaten anything that was **unclean.** The voice declared, **"Don't treat as unclean what God has cleansed"**[3] (v. 15). Three times this occurred before the container disappeared into the sky. What was this all about?

The ceremonies of the Mosaic law were designed to minutely regulate the life of the Israelite. His clothing, food, and the like were all prescribed. This was to show him that he was to follow God's requirements; all else was unclean. The idea that there were health reasons for not eating certain foods is foolish. The distinctions were entirely arbitrary. There would have been no less a health hazard in Peter's day than there would have been earlier on. Peter was not being advised to do an unhealthy thing.

The point of the clean/unclean regulations was simply to teach God's people that His way was the right way, and all others were wrong. Visible distinctions made this point. Along with that, they taught the believer that

---

[1] A place that was frequently used for this purpose. Palestinian roofs were flat.

[2] Not a favorite verse for either animal rights people or vegetarians!

[3] Cf. I Timothy 4:3-5; Mark 7:19; Romans 14:14.

16 This happened three times, then immediately the container was taken up into the sky.

God had a right to regulate his life and that throughout every day he should be concerned in all that he does to choose God's way rather than any other. To fail to understand that was to miss the purposes of the regulations.

These regulations had been imposed upon Israel in the way that strict regulations used to be placed upon minor children in our society (before Dr. Spock). They were for the childhood of the people of God, not for the maturity about which God speaks in Galatians chapters 3 and 4. Peter was being shown that the former age of immaturity was passing. The whole Mosaic system that pertained to the Israelites was to be abandoned. The true sacrifice had been made; Jesus had come and died. All those things that typified Him and the regulations that set apart God's people from all others were to be laid aside. A new people of God who would be treated like adults was being formed. And it would be composed of Gentiles as well as converted Jews. Prior to this time, in Israel's immaturity, the Gentile himself was considered unclean. He ate foods that were forbidden to Israelites. As a consequence, they could not eat with him. But that was all to give way to a new era in which spiritual cleanness and uncleanness were the rule rather than ritual cleanness and uncleanness. Gentiles were to be accepted as clean. They were to be taken into the membership of the church. That was the meaning of the vision.

There are times when counselees must abandon their immature ways. Those who have been steeped in legalism (there are many such who find a need to be counseled) will have difficulty abandoning those regulations of men that have been required by various churches. Unlike the Mosaic regulations, they never were correct in God's sight. But like them, people hold tenaciously to them. The biblical counselor will probably hear objections when he attempts to get them to see in counseling that these rules are part of their problem (as they so often are). Like Peter, they may have to be convinced. It may take three—or more—confrontations with biblical truth to disabuse them of their former allegiance to such things. The point must be made that the New Testament is entirely what the Old Testament was designed to lead men to—a spiritual religion[1] (cf.

---

[1] Even in Old Testament times the Jews were to see beyond the symbol to its significance. The tragedy is that so many did not.

17 While Peter was inwardly wondering what to make of this vision, just then the men that Cornelius had sent arrived at the gate and asked for directions to Simon's house.

18 They called out, asking if the Simon, who was called Peter, was staying there.

19 So while Peter was still pondering over the vision, the Spirit said to him,

> See here, three men are looking for you.

20 > Get up and go down and accompany them without hesitation, because I have sent them.

21 So Peter went down and said to the men, "All right, I'm the one you are looking for; what is it that you have come for?"

22 They said,

> Cornelius, a centurion who is just and fears God, who is well spoken of by the whole Jewish nation, was directed by a holy angel to send for you to come to his house and to listen to what you have to say.

23 So he invited them in to be his guests.

The next day he got up and went off with them, and some of the brothers from Joppa went with him.

24 The next day he arrived at Caesarea. Cornelius had been expecting them and had called together his relatives and close friends.

25 When Peter entered, Cornelius fell down at his feet and worshiped him.

John 4:24).

At any rate, the Gentiles were to be accepted into the church without first becoming Jews or submitting to all of the rules and regulations of the ceremonial law of Moses. That is what Peter was being shown. As Peter was trying to figure out the vision, Cornelius' emissaries arrived at the house where Peter was and asked for him (vv. 17, 18). The Spirit spoke to Peter and told him to go with them because He had sent them (v. 20). Peter greeted them and asked what they wanted (v. 21). They told him about the angel's visit to Cornelius and that the centurion was waiting to hear what Peter had to say. Peter, the servants, the soldier, and some Christians from Joppa went the next day to Caesarea. Cornelius called for a gathering of his family and friends to meet with Peter (v. 24).

Cornelius was a man who was not only concerned about himself but also wanted his whole family and his friends to benefit from what God was about to reveal to him through Peter. A genuine Christian will want others to know God's good ways. When you have been a blessing to a

26 But Peter made him get up and said, "Get up. I too am a man."

27 And he talked to him as they entered, where he found many had gathered.

28 Then he said to them,

> You know that it is unlawful for a Jewish man to associate with or to visit a foreigner. Yet God has shown me that I shouldn't call any man common or unclean.

29 So when I was called, I came without argument. Let me ask, then, why you called for me.

30 Then Cornelius said,

> Four days ago, about this hour—at three o'clock in the afternoon—I was praying in my house when, then and there, a man in bright clothing stood before me.

31 He said, "Cornelius, your prayer has been heard, and your charity has been remembered by God.

32 Send to Joppa for Simon who is called Peter; he is staying in Simon the tanner's house that is by the sea."

33 So at once I sent word to you, and you were kind enough to come. Now, then, we are all here present before God to hear everything that the Lord commanded you.

34 Then Peter opened his mouth and said,

> I can see now that God isn't a respecter of persons.

35 Instead, in every nation, whoever fears Him and practices righteousness is acceptable to Him.

---

counselee, more than likely he will want to tell others about it, might even recommend that others come for help, and may be willing to allow you to use his testimony of what God has done for him when dealing with others who are dubious.

Cornelius fell down before Peter and worshipped him. Peter forbade this saying, **"Get up. I too am a man."** We are told that many gathered. Presumably Cornelius had a large family and a number of friends. Here were the makings of the first Gentile church! Peter had by now had enough time to consider the vision. The Spirit of God also helped him to understand. So as he spoke, he told about the vision of the animals and disclosed its meaning: **"God has shown me that I shouldn't call any man common or unclean".** In making the visit to Cornelius and staying in this home, Peter was making a decisive break with the past in his own life. His act was symbolic of what was happening in redemptive history: the old order was giving way to the new. Peter then asked Cornelius why he had sent for him, and Cornelius told Peter his story (vv. 30-33). Peter is

36	The message is the one that He sent to the sons of Israel, preaching peace through Jesus Christ—He is Lord of everything.
37	You know what happened throughout all Judea, starting at Galilee after the baptism that John preached—
38	how God anointed Jesus of Nazareth with the Holy Spirit and power, how He went about doing good and healing all those who were overpowered by the devil, because God was with Him.
39	We are witnesses of everything that He did in the Jews' country and in Jerusalem. They killed Him by hanging Him on a tree,
40	but God raised Him up on the third day and had Him appear,
41	not to all the people, but to us who were previously chosen by God to be witnesses. We ate and drank with Him after He rose from the dead.
42	He ordered us to preach to the people and to testify that He is the One Whom God designated to be Judge of the living and the dead.
43	To Him all the prophets bear witness that everybody who believes in Him will receive forgiveness of sins through His name.

---

further enlightened by this and addressed the group in another of the Spirit-inspired utterances recorded by Luke (vv. 34-43). In this address he declared that the Old Testament prophecies of the gospel going to the nations had been fulfilled: "**I can now see that God isn't a respecter of persons. Instead, in every nation, whoever fears Him and practices righteousness is acceptable to Him**." Then he preached the gospel. Beginning with John the Baptist's ministry, he told the story of the coming of Christ to die for guilty sinners. He declared that he was a **witness** of all that had happened and gave evidence of the resurrection (vv. 40-42). He showed how Jesus was the fulfillment of all the Old Testament promises and how all who believed in Him would receive the forgiveness of sins.

This sermon contains very valuable truths for evangelism. For one thing, Peter makes it clear that true faith (**fearing** God) is always accompanied by **righteous** living. He is in complete accord with James. Jesus is set forth as the **Lord of everything**. This truth is often muted today. In addition the apostolic **witness** to Christ is set forth as the basis for faith. God's **judgment** of the world is also presented in this message (as in Acts 17). Seldom, today, is that a part of the evangelistic approach. In other words, modern day evangelism could be greatly informed by this first presentation of the good news to a Gentile audience. Counselors, instructing their counselees about how to witness to others, could take a leaf from

71

44 While Peter was still speaking these words, the Holy Spirit fell on all those who heard his message.

45 The believers from the circumcision who had come with Peter were astounded that the gift of the Holy Spirit had been poured out on the Gentiles too

46 (they heard them speaking in various languages and exalting God). Then Peter said,

47 "Nobody could refuse water to baptize these people who have received the Holy Spirit just as we have, could he?"

48 So he ordered them to be baptized in the name of Jesus Christ. Then they asked him to stay for a few days.

Peter's book as well.

As Peter was unlocking the door to the church for the Gentiles by the second use of the keys Jesus gave to him, **the Holy Spirit fell on** the group that was assembled. Peter and his friends from Joppa were amazed at this (v. 45). They heard the repetition of the Pentecostal experience of speaking in tongues. This made it clear to Peter and his friends that there was no difference between the Jews and the Gentiles. Peter then included them in the church, apart from their becoming Jews first, by saying that they too should be **baptized**. The inclusion of the Gentiles was a momentous step forward for the infant church. It would then have an international impact. No longer could the apostles look at what was happening as merely an event in Israel. The new order had dawned; the old was passing. It would cause problems for the Jewish church, as we shall see, but they would have to learn from this event in which God was clearly bringing about a radical change.

God doesn't spare His churches. He leads them providentially into problems and expects them to handle them as He has told them and shown them in the Scriptures. As they follow His word He imparts wisdom and strength to do so. There is never an excuse for a congregation to throw up its hands and say "We're helpless!" Indeed, in the early church's life we see church members maturing through this process.

CHAPTER 11

1 Now the apostles and the brothers throughout Judea heard that the Gentiles also had received God's Word.

2 But when Peter went up to Jerusalem, those who were zealous for circumcision argued with him, saying,

3 "You visited and ate with uncircumcised men!"

4 So Peter began and explained to them in order, saying,

5   I was in the city of Joppa praying, and in a trance I saw a vision of a container, like a huge sheet, being let down from the sky by its four corners; and it came down to me.

6   I looked into it and saw animals of the earth, wild beasts, reptiles and birds of the sky.

7   Then I also heard a voice saying to me, "Get up, Peter! Kill and eat them."

8   I said, "Oh no, Lord! A common or unclean thing hasn't ever entered my mouth."

9   But the voice from the sky spoke a second time, "What God has cleansed, don't you call common."

10   This happened three times, and then everything was pulled up again into the sky.

11   Then, at that very moment, three men arrived at the gate of the house where I was, who had been sent to me from Caesarea.

The eleventh chapter grows out of the tenth. The word was soon out that Peter had eaten with uncircumcised Gentiles and had admitted them to Christian baptism and membership in the church. Jews in the Jerusalem church wanted to know how this could be (vv. 1-3). They too were being stretched. Some thought he had done wrong and **argued with him**. So, Peter retold the circumstances that were related in chapter 10, at the conclusion of which he asked, **"who was I to stand in God's way?"** (vv. 4-17). The uproar that Peter's action in Caesarea had at first occasioned died down after his explanation (v. 18), and the church **glorified God**. With Peter, they concluded that **God had granted the Gentiles the repentance that leads to life**. That phrase is an interesting way to express what Peter had called **a message by which you and your household can be saved** (v. 14). In spite of those who teach otherwise, it is clear that **repentance** is a part of the change we call conversion or salvation. Never forget this in discussing these matters with counselees. Repentance means a change of mind (Greek, *metanoia*) that leads to a change of life (Hebrew, *shuv*).

12   The Spirit told me not to have the slightest hesitation about going with them. And these six brothers also went with me, and we went into the man's house.

13   And he related to us how he had seen the angel standing in his house and saying, "Send to Joppa for Simon who is called Peter.

14   He has a message to speak to you by which you and your whole household can be saved."

15   As I began to speak, the Holy Spirit fell on them just as on us at the beginning.

16   Then I remembered the Lord's Word, how He said, "John indeed baptized with water, but you will be baptized with the Holy Spirit."

17   So if God gave them a gift equal to the one that He gave us when we believed on the Lord Jesus Christ, who was I to stand in God's way?

18   When they heard this they quieted down, and they glorified God, saying, "So then, God has granted the Gentiles the repentance that leads to life!"

19   Now those who had been scattered about by the persecution that arose in connection with Stephen went as far as Phoenicia, Cyprus and Antioch. But they didn't tell the message to anybody but Jews.

20   But some of the Cypriots and Cyrenians, when they came to Antioch, also spoke to the Greeks, preaching the Lord Jesus.

At first, most of those who had been scattered abroad (cf. chapter 8) told only other **Jews** about the gospel (v. 19). They, too, had no idea that the Gentiles would be admitted into the church. However, some from Cyprus and Cyrene did tell some Greeks at Antioch, and a **number believed and turned to the Lord**[1] (v. 21). Things were happening. The church had burst its early Jewish fetters never again to be confined to one nation or group of people. News of the conversion of Greeks in Antioch reached Jerusalem. The church there sent Barnabas to investigate (vv. 22-24). This was a prudent measure. To assure themselves that the news was accurate and that the message that was preached to the Greeks had not been garbled was important. Sometimes people accept stories of conversions without any proper investigation. We hear of presidents, celebrities of every sort, and great numbers of people in foreign lands being con-

---

[1] The phrase **turned to the Lord** expresses the meaning of the Hebrew *shuv* just mentioned in the previous paragraph.

21 The Lord's hand was with them, and a large number believed and turned to the Lord.

22 News of this reached the ears of the church in Jerusalem, so they sent Barnabas off to Antioch.

23 When he arrived and saw the results of God's grace, he was glad and encouraged all of them to remain true to the Lord with determined hearts.

24 He was a good man who was full of the Holy Spirit and faith. And a satisfying number of people was added to the Lord.

25 Then Barnabas went to Tarsus to look for Saul,

---

verted. Many of these reports, when investigated, turn out to be inaccurate. Or *what* the person(s) believed turns out to be something other than the gospel. Counselors, therefore, will be careful to investigate not only what they hear about conversions and about supposed radical changes in counselees and others.

Barnabas was favorably impressed by what he found. He spent some time **encouraging** the new believers and urged them to **remain true to the Lord**. Barnabas' character is mentioned and his work in Antioch was said to be fruitful (v. 24). The church grew under his ministry. It is interesting that we see no hesitancy on Barnabas' part to preach to the Greeks. It was part of his lifestyle to be an encourager, and that is precisely what we see him doing from the outset. Every counselor needs to learn what it means to encourage counselees. A large part of the work of counseling involves encouraging others. People who come to counseling are often very discouraged. They have been here and there, done this and that, but all has failed. It is important to encourage them, giving them hope, since when they finally determine to try what the Lord's Word says, there is every reason for them to be encouraged. Encourage them not to trust themselves or even you, but in the Word of the One Who never fails.

Evidently, Barnabas was also stretched and began to see the potential for spreading the message far and wide. He knew that he would need help to do so. So, remembering the remarkable conversion of Saul and knowing what God had told him about becoming a **vessel** to carry the message to the Gentiles, he went off to Tarsus to find Saul (v. 25). Counselors need to encourage others to enter the gospel ministry when they discover the gifts for ministry in their lives. Never forget that your counselee, for all his problems, has a place in Christ's church. Part of the task of counseling is to encourage counselees to go back to the church and to take up responsibilities in it that they have left behind (or never assumed)—including urging some who should to enter the ministry. Barnabas brought Saul

26   and when he found him, he brought him to Antioch. So it was that for one whole year they met with the church and taught a large number of people, and it was in Antioch that the disciples were first called Christians.

27   During this time prophets came down from Jerusalem to Antioch.

28   One of them, named Agabus, stood up and revealed by the Spirit that there would be a great famine throughout the entire Mediterranean world. (It took place in Claudius' reign.)

29   So the disciples, as each was able from his means, determined to send contributions to help their brothers living in Jerusalem.

30   And they did so, sending them to the elders by the hand of Barnabas and Saul.

---

back to Antioch where for a year the two of them ministered, teaching a **large number** about Christ. During this remarkable ministry at Antioch, believers were **first called Christians** (v. 26).

Some **prophets** from Jerusalem came to Antioch while Saul and Barnabas were ministering there. One of the prophets named **Agabus** revealed that there would be a great **famine**. So the disciples, recognizing the poverty of their fellow Christians in Jerusalem, raised money and sent it to them. Barnabas and Saul were designated to carry the funds, which they did. This chapter is transitional and helps lead us into the story of Saul, who became Paul. Chapter 12 will finally wrap up the picture at Jerusalem and take us into territories beyond.[1]

---

[1] Though in Chapter fifteen we shall return briefly to attend the Jerusalem synod.

CHAPTER 12

1 About this time King Herod set about to mistreat some of those who belonged to the church.

2   Accordingly, he killed James, John's brother, with the sword,

3   and when he saw that this pleased the Jews, he went on to arrest Peter too. (This was during the days of the Unleavened Bread.)

4   He seized him and put him in prison and handed him over to four squads of soldiers to guard him, intending after the Passover to bring him out to the people.

The **Herod** mentioned in verse 1 is Herod Agrippa. Herod did everything he could to cater to the Jews so as to remain in power. Rome did not like disturbances in the provinces. Evidently, he found a way to appease the Jews: to abuse Christians (v. 1). When he discovered how much killing James the brother of **John** the apostle had pleased the Jews, he determined to eliminate **Peter** also (vv. 2, 3). He had him arrested and held until the feast of Unleavened Bread was completed. At this time, **when the Passover**[1] was over, he planned to **bring** Peter **out to the people** (vv. 3-5; the way that Jesus was brought before them as a spectacle). Counselees who look at circumstances fail to realize that God has His own agenda which, more often than not, does not correspond very closely to man's. Looking at the circumstances, you would have said, "Well, Peter is as good as dead." He wasn't. God had other plans. Don't second guess the future. God's answer to prayer, as we shall see, made the difference. The church was praying for Peter; God freed him and delivered him from harm.[2]

When a counselee says, "There's no hope," counter that. You might say something like this: "Do you mean that the situation is too far gone for God to do anything about it?" Drive home the need for faith. Don't promise that God will deliver, or speculate about how He might do so (you do not know the future). But you *can* say that God, in answer to prayer, may do all sorts of unexpected things to change the circumstances

---

[1] The King James version says "intending after Easter." That never was a proper translation; the text in 1611, just as it does today, reads "Passover." Those who think that the King James Version is so accurate and free from interpolations, need to consider this very prejudicial translation.

[2] The expression "prayer changes things" is wrong. It is God Who changes them, as He often does.

77

5   So Peter was kept in prison.
Now the church earnestly prayed to God for him,
6   and during the very night before Herod was going to bring him out, Peter was sleeping between two soldiers, bound with two chains, with sentries in front of the door guarding the prison.
7   Suddenly, an angel from the Lord appeared, and a light shined in the cell. He poked Peter's side and awakened him and said, "Get up quickly." And the chains fell from his hands.
8   Then the angel said to him, "Get dressed and put your sandals on." So he did. And he said to him, "Wrap your coat around you and follow me."
9   Then he left with Peter following him. He didn't realize that what the angel was doing was real; he thought he was seeing a vision.
10 They passed the first and the second guards and came to the iron gate leading to the city. On its own it opened for them. They went out, and when they had gone one street's distance, all at once the angel left him.

and the people who face them. Take the following as an example. There is a husband who, up until now, has never kept a job. He gets into brawls with his superiors and is fired—even though he is otherwise a good worker. He has just lost his third job this year. His wife says, "I've given up." You say, "But you shouldn't." She says, "He'll never change." You ask, "How do you know that?" She says, "Well, this has been going on for ten years without change." You reply, "OK. Let's grant that. But though this may have happened a hundred times, who is to say that it will happen 101 times? After all, this is the first time you have asked God to help. Don't you expect Him to answer your prayers? Don't you think that God can make a difference?"

Verse 5 makes it clear that **the church earnestly prayed for** Peter. And God answered that prayer—just when it looked like all was lost. The night before Herod was going to bring Peter out, an **angel** awakened him, unchained him, led him out of prison, and set him free (vv. 6-9). Peter could hardly believe what was happening; **he thought he was seeing a vision**. He wasn't; it was for real! He realized this only when he was out of the prison and had walked some distance along the street (vv. 10, 11). It is hard sometimes to believe all that God does for us. If we were to look back over the past year or two and recall where we were and what we were expecting to happen to us, and then remember what really did happen, most believers would have to say that God has done far more for us than we could have ever dreamed. It wouldn't be bad at times to ask a counselee to do that very thing. He might be amazed at how God has protected him from harm and guided his steps into pleasant paths. This is *if* he has been praying.

11 Then Peter came to himself and said,

> Now I know that the Lord has really sent His angel and delivered me from Herod's hand and from everything that the Jewish people were expecting.

12 When he realized what had happened, he went to the house of Mary, the mother of John (who is called Mark), where many were gathered together, praying.

13 When he knocked at the gateway door, a maid named Rhoda came to answer.

14 But when she recognized Peter's voice, in her joy she didn't open the gate but ran in and announced that Peter was standing at the gate.

15 They said to her, "You're crazy!" Yet she insisted that it was so. Then they said, "It's his angel."

16 But Peter continued to knock. When they opened the gate, they saw him and were astounded.

Peter went to the house of **Mary**, John **Mark's** mother, where the **brothers** were meeting to pray for him. He knocked on the gate and **Rhoda**, the servant girl, came to answer the knock. Seeing Peter, she was so happy that she forgot to open the gate. Instead she rushed inside to tell the others. Notice that though they had been praying for Peter's release, they all said things like, "**You're crazy!**" and, "**It's his angel**" (vv. 12-15). They were like the farming congregation who came to church to pray for rain and nobody brought an umbrella! Do we *really* believe even though we may pray **earnestly**? Fervor and faith are not the same thing.[1] Stress this to counselees.

Poor Peter, standing outside, continued to knock until they finally let him in. It says that when they recognized that it was really Peter at the door they were **astounded**. God loves to astound us. We should believe this and expect that He will answer prayer—in His time and His way which, we may be sure, is always better than ours. The answer is often so remarkable that we can hardly believe it.

Peter quieted them down and then described what had happened (v. 17). Peter then told them to report to James (the brother of Jesus) and the others what God had done, after which he left the area. We do not know where Peter went, but that is because he was hiding out from Herod. The excitement at the prison must have been something to see. "How could he have escaped?" Blaming them for the escape, Herod executed the guards and left for Caesarea (vv. 18, 19).

---

[1] "Fervor" can be nothing more than an emotional experience.

17 He motioned with his hand for silence and then described to them how the Lord had led him out of the prison. He said, "Report this to James and to the brothers." Then he left and went to another place.

18 Now when the day dawned, there was no small stir among the soldiers about what had become of Peter.

19 When Herod looked for him but couldn't find him, he interrogated the guards and ordered them to be led away to execution. Then he left Judea and went to Caesarea, where he stayed for awhile.

20 Now he was quite angry with the residents of Tyre and Sidon, so they came to him unitedly, and by persuading Blastus, the king's personal attendant, they asked for peace, because their country got its food from the king's country.

21 So on a set day, Herod arrayed himself with kingly clothing, took his seat on the throne and delivered a speech to them.

22 The mob shouted, "This is a god's voice, not a human voice!"

23 Instantly an angel from the Lord struck him, because he didn't give God the glory: he was eaten by worms and died.

24 Now the Lord's Word continued to grow and increase.

25 And Barnabas and Saul returned from Jerusalem after completing their mission, bringing with them John who was called Mark.

The incident that follows tells of the horrible end of Herod (vv. 20-23). The residents of Tyre and Sidon were afraid of Herod, so they persuaded his personal attendant to sue for peace. After all, they were dependent upon Herod's country for food. Herod arrayed himself with kingly clothing (Josephus says with a shining silver robe) and delivered an oration to the Phoenician people. To butter him up, the crowd shouted, "**This is a god's voice, not a human voice!**" But an angel struck him because he accepted this praise rather than giving God the glory. And he was **eaten by worms**[1] and died.

In His time, God will vindicate His own. This bloody king, who would willingly trade the lives of God's people for his own popularity, deserved nothing less than the vengeance of God. If it is not meted out fully in this life, and if a person does not repent and believe the gospel, the rest of his punishment will be given in hell. It is not our part to take vengeance. Vengeance belongs to God. All who attempt to take vengeance into their own hands err. God says, "Make room for vengeance." He is coming in His time and way to mete it out (cf. Romans 12:14ff.).

---

[1] Some think that this was an expression used for any sudden, catastrophic illness. But it could have been literal.

CHAPTER 13

1 Now in the church at Antioch there were prophets and teachers: Barnabas, Simeon (called Niger), Lucius (from Cyrene), Manaen (a close friend of Herod the tetrarch) and Saul.

2 As they were worshiping the Lord and fasting, the Holy Spirit said, "Set apart Barnabas and Saul for the work to which I have called them."

3 Then, after they had fasted and prayed, they laid their hands on them and sent them off.

The base of operations of the Gentile **church** had been established in **Antioch** of Syria. A list of the **prophets and teachers** in this church is listed in verse 1. Interestingly, Barnabas and Saul are included among them. They had become recognized teachers in this expanding church which by now probably comprised several congregations with one central eldership that governed them. Doubtless through one of the prophets a message came to the church to **set apart Barnabas and Saul** to a new **work:** the work of missions. Consequently, after fasting and praying, the leaders of the church **laid hands on them and sent them off** (v. 3). The official nature of the act is prominent. The early church did not simply act in a loose manner when conducting its affairs. It did things in an orderly fashion. There was organization, not mere improvisation.

One of the sad things in our day is that the church is being led by all sorts of persons who, unlike Barnabas and Saul, were never called or ordained by the church of Jesus Christ. They operate outside of church authority. Without the official sanction of Christ's church, without the **laying on of hands** (ordination), they dare to tell preachers and congregations what to do. This is particularly true in the area of counseling. People who have studied psychology in universities boldly criticize preachers that God and the church have called and attempt to usurp their tasks. The church is God's. Jesus Christ is King and Head. He is the One to rule it. He does things in a decent and orderly fashion—His way. No one can buy his way (as we saw earlier) into leadership in the church. Today, however, it seems that if you have celebrity status or money to acquire radio and television coverage, it is quite possible to purchase power in the church by means of these things. The orderly way to enter Christ's ministry, however, is for the **Holy Spirit** to call and the **church** to confirm that call as we see God and the church doing here. The interesting thing is that Barnabas and Saul are said to have been **sent out by the *church*** (v. 3) but also

4 So then, being sent out by the Holy Spirit, they went down to Seleucia and from there sailed away to Cyprus.

5 When they arrived at Salamis, they proclaimed God's Word in the Jewish synagogs. And they had John as an assistant.

6 When they had gone through the whole island as far as Paphos, they came upon a man whose name was Bar-Jesus; he was a magician and a Jewish false prophet.

7 He was with the proconsul Sergius Paulus, an intelligent man, who summoned Barnabas and Saul and sought to hear God's Word.

8 Now Elymas the magician (that is the translation of his name) opposed them and tried to turn the proconsul away from the faith.

9 But Saul (who also is called Paul), filled with the Holy Spirit, looked straight at him and said,

---

sent out by the *Holy Spirit* (v. 4). In other words, the Holy Spirit works through the church, not apart from it. That is what needs to be emphasized to those who want to operate outside of it. There is no place for ministry that is not under the church's authority (either directly or indirectly).

Arriving in Cyprus, the preachers began to teach in the synagogs there. And **John** Mark was with them as an **assistant**. The preached from one end of the island to the other. In **Paphos** they encountered a Jewish **false prophet** who performed **magic**. There must have been quite a bit of this sort of thing going on (remember Simon Magus). This man, **Bar-Jesus** ("son of Jesus"), had attempted to keep the local **proconsul, Sergius Paulus**, from listening to the preachers, fearing he might put his trust in Jesus Christ. (This, of course, would free him from the bonds of superstition and magic.) But the proconsul summoned the new preachers to hear what they had to say (vv. 5-8). The proconsul was, Luke says, **an intelligent man.**[1] Probably, as such, he was interested in learning all he could about the message that was being proclaimed throughout Cyprus. Intelligence alone does not lead to faith; but if the Spirit of God is working through intelligence, a good outcome can be rapid and quite impressive.

Saul (he now is introduced to the reader by his second, Roman name **Paul**), under the power and inspiration of the Holy Spirit (v. 9), excoriates Bar-Jesus. He calls him (accurately) a **son of the devil**, says that he is **full of deceit and fraud** and characterizes him as an **enemy of every kind of righteousness**. Obviously, because he was a **magician** and a **false prophet** Paul's words nailed him. They were right on the money. He was

---

[1] Not necessarily highly educated.

10   You son of the devil, full of every kind of deceit and fraud, you
        enemy of every kind of righteousness; won't you ever stop mak-
        ing the Lord's straight roads crooked?

11   Now, see, the Lord's hand is on you; you will be blind and unable
        to see the sun for a time.

Instantly, a mist and darkness fell upon him, and he went about seeking
people to lead him by the hand.

12   Then, when the proconsul saw what had happened, he believed, and he
was amazed at the Lord's teaching.

---

engaged in **making the Lord's straight paths crooked**. They were twisting God's Word (the Old Testament) so as to teach things that were contrary to it. People, as a result, were led astray on **crooked roads**, rather
than the **straight roads** set forth in Scripture. That is what Satan did in the
beginning; and that is what he is still in the business of doing. That is what
false prophets (there are many today) still do. They set forth as *God's,*
paths that are not His at all. In other words, they defraud people by teaching ideas and practices that are really a twisting of the truth (cf. II Peter
3:16). Counselors who are full of the **Spirit** will denounce such ways.
Unlike Paul (with Luke, we will call him such from now on), there are too
many who are unwilling to confront and speak the truth about those who
twist the truth. It is time for counselors to stand up for God's Word against
the many misrepresentations of it that are found in our society.

By the power of God, Bar-Jesus was struck **blind** for a time according to the word of Paul. The **proconsul** saw what had happened, and he
believed the gospel. He was **amazed**, however, not so much at the miracle, but (as it says) **at the Lord's teaching**.[1] What happened to the magician we are not told. The important thing to see is that a man of the stature
and intelligence of Sergius Paulus could readily recognize and distinguish
true from false teaching when he heard it. The Scripture (which today is
the repository of the apostolic message) presents God's **straight roads**.
That is what the proconsul (along with intelligent counselees) was able to
see. For those not so intelligent, you may have to spell out matters in other
ways. The alacrity with which the proconsul came to faith exhibits his
intelligence in responding to God's grace (vv. 11, 12).

John Mark returned to Jerusalem when they reached Perga. Why, we
don't know, but mentioning it here sets up later comments about John
Mark. Next on the trip was Pisidian Antioch (vv. 13, 14). Here Paul and

---

[1] Though it is possible that the word **teaching** is used here to cover both.

13 Now Paul and his companions set sail from Paphos and came to Perga in Pamphylia. But John left them and returned to Jerusalem.

14 Then from Perga they went on to Pisidian Antioch. And on the Sabbath day they went into the synagog and sat down.

15 After the reading of the Law and the Prophets the synagog rulers sent this word to them: "Brothers, if you have any word of encouragement for the people, speak up."

16 So Paul stood up and motioned with his hand and said,
Men of Israel and you God-fearing Gentiles, listen.

17 The God of this people Israel chose our fathers and exalted the people during the time when they were foreigners in the land of Egypt, and with His arm raised high led them out of it.

18 For about a forty-year period of time He put up with them in the wilderness.

19 Then, after He destroyed seven nations in the land of Canaan, He gave them their land as an inheritance for about four hundred and fifty years.

20 After that He gave them judges until Samuel the prophet.

21 Next, they asked for a king, and God gave them Saul, Kish's son, who was from Benjamin's tribe, and he reigned forty years.

22 When He had removed him, He raised up David for their king, about whom He testified, saying, **"In David, Jesse's son, I have found a man after My own heart**, who will do everything I want him to."

Barnabas attended a **synagog** service on the Sabbath. The leaders recognized that these were brothers who had a message and, according to Jewish synagog custom, they invited them to speak (v. 15). Paul, adopting the Greek style, **stood up** to speak (v. 16). Palestinian teaching was done sitting down. Luke is quite conscious of such matters and shows how Paul adapted to his audiences. Counselors should be aware of such details when working with people from varied backgrounds, and do all they can to adapt. You certainly don't speak to a Sergius Paulus the same way you would speak to a redneck if you are wise.

In verses 17 through 41, we have Paul's first recorded sermon. It is reminiscent of Stephen's address, sketching the history of the people of Israel so as to lead up to the coming, death and resurrection of Christ. Note, on the matter of adaptation, that Paul knew his audience. He addresses not only the Jews, but the **God-fearers** (vv. 16, 26) as well. These were Gentiles who believed in Yahweh as the true God, accepted imageless worship, trusted in the inspiration of the Bible, observed the

23   From this man's descendants God has brought to Israel the Savior Jesus.

24   Before His coming John had preached a baptism of repentance to all the people of Israel.

25   Then, as John completed his course he said, "What do you think I am? I am not He. Rather, One is coming after me Whose sandals I am not worthy to untie."

26   Brothers, sons of Abraham's family, and those among you who fear God, to us the message of this salvation has been sent forth.

27   Those who live in Jerusalem and their rulers didn't recognize Him or the prophets' words that are read every Sabbath, and fulfilled them by condemning Him.

28   Though they could find no grounds for His death, they asked Pilate to destroy Him.

29   When they had finished doing everything that was written about Him, they took Him down from the tree and laid Him in a tomb.

30   But God raised Him from the dead,

31   and for many days He appeared to those who came up with Him from Galilee to Jerusalem, who now are His witnesses to the people.

32   We announce to you the good news that what God promised to the fathers,

---

Sabbath, and probably kept some or all of the dietary laws. They attended services at the synagog, but had not yet become circumcised Jews. Throughout this sermon Paul is angling for both Jews and Greeks. In the end, he catches more of the latter than of the former.

The lection for the day included passages to which Paul alluded in his sermon. This shows his great knowledge of the Bible and, again, a flexibility to adapt to the circumstances at hand. All of his quotations were from the Septuagint (the Greek translation of the Hebrew Old Testament that was made in Alexandria). That was another clear instance of adaptation.[1] This ability to adapt, if anything, is more readily needed in counseling than in preaching. A counselor must be able to locate and use any passage of the Bible that is appropriate to the discussion as it proceeds. He cannot plan and execute a counseling session according to predetermined factors as he might in preaching; he must be able to move

---

[1] Paul didn't mind using more than one translation. Those who confine themselves to a version that is written in outdated English, as some counselors do, are perpetuating an unbiblical error.

33 He has fulfilled to us, their children, by raising Jesus as it is written in the second Psalm: **You are My Son; today I have become Your Father**.

34 That He raised Him from the dead never to return to decay is stated like this: **I will give you the holy** blessings **that were assured to David.**

35 It is for this reason that He also says in another Psalm, **You won't let Your Holy One see decay.**

36 David, after he had served God's purpose in his own generation, fell asleep and was added to his fathers and saw decay.

37 But the One Whom God raised didn't see decay.

38 So then, let it be known to you brothers that through this Man forgiveness of sins is announced to you,

39 and by Him everybody who believes is justified in everything in regard to which he couldn't be justified by Moses' law.

40 So then, watch out that what the prophets spoke about doesn't come upon you:

41 **See you scoffers; wonder and perish**
because I will work a work in your days—
a work that you simply won't believe
if somebody tells you about it.

42 As they left, the people begged them to talk further about these things on the next Sabbath.

---

with data as he acquires it and with the ongoing responses of the counselee. He therefore needs to develop a high degree of biblical flexibility that, while never adapting the message, is always adapted to other factors. Missionary preaching is the closest to counseling because in the missionary setting the unexpected often occurs. Counselors, like missionaries, must learn to expect the unexpected.

The object of Paul's message was to show how God had always provided more and more good for His people, culminating in the giving of His Son, Who is the greatest Good. They, therefore, should gratefully trust His Son. Luke recorded both the short and long term results of this sermon. The immediate results showed that the sermon was quite successful: Paul and Barnabas were invited back to speak again (v. 42), there were private discussions (v. 43), and there was an amazing amount of Gentile interest (vv. 43, 44). And many believed. But when the Jews saw the interest of so many in the city, they became envious of Paul and Barnabas. Outsiders were stealing the show (v. 45; cf. III John). So they argued

43　When the congregation broke up, many of the Jews and of the wor-shiping proselytes followed Paul and Barnabas, who spoke to them and urged them to persevere by God's grace.

44　The next Sabbath almost the whole city was gathered to hear God's Word.

45　But when the Jews saw the crowds they were filled with jealousy and contradicted what Paul said, and blasphemed him.

46　And Paul and Barnabas, speaking boldly, said,

> It was necessary to speak God's Word to you first. Since you thrust it away and don't consider yourselves worthy of eternal life, we are turning to the Gentiles.

47　　Now this is what the Lord has commanded us:
> **I have set you as a light for the Gentiles**
> **so that you may bring salvation to the ends of the earth.**

48　When the Gentiles heard this, they were glad and glorified the Lord's Word, and as many as were destined for eternal life believed.

49　So the Lord's Word spread throughout the whole region.

50　But the Jews incited the devout women of high standing and the lead-ing men of the city and stirred up persecution against Paul and Barnabas and drove them from their borders.

---

with Paul and blasphemed him. The preachers then said, **Since you thrust [God's Word] away and don't consider yourselves worthy of eternal life, we are turning to the Gentiles.** And they quoted Scripture to back up their action (v. 47). Many Gentiles **gladly** believed and the gospel spread throughout the region (vv. 48, 49). When ministering the Word, there is a time to turn from those who will not hear to those who will. Counselors sometimes continue too long, pleading, urging, even begging counselees. There is point when it becomes apparent that a person is bent on resisting God's Word (that, notice, is the touchstone) and there is no longer a point to wasting time with him.[1] Spend your time with those who **gladly** hear the Word.

The opposition of the unbelieving Jews was so strong that they were able to drive the apostles from the city. Noteworthy is the influence of some of the **women** who were opposed to them (v. 50).[2] Paul and Barna-bas then did as the Lord had directed: they wiped the dust off their feet as

---

[1] Of course, counselees, as members of the church, are entitled to the privileges of church discipline. In turning from them it is assumed that discipline has been adequately exercised and they have not responded positively.

[2] Women arrayed for or against Christianity can be a force to reckon with!

51   So they shook the dust from their feet against them and went to Iconium.

52   And the disciples were filled with joy and with the Holy Spirit.

---

a sign that they wanted nothing more to do with them (or even with dust from their city) and went on to Iconium. But the **disciples** who had been left behind were a happy group who rejoiced in Christ and their newfound faith. The negative response of the Jews was so strong because it was motivated by **envy**. We have seen already how powerful a motivating emotion this can be. It can lead to murder. More division in the church and animosity among believers stems from envy than from doctrinal differences. Whenever you encounter envy in a counselee, always do two things. First, watch out for his responses toward you; they might be very strong. Second, warn him of the dire consequences of envy and urge him to deal with it. He may need a great deal of help.

CHAPTER 14

1 Now at Iconium, in the same way they entered the Jewish synagog, and spoke so that a great number of both Jews and Greeks believed.
2   But the disbelieving Jews stirred up the Gentiles and poisoned their minds against the brothers.

The gospel was delivered to the Jews first, then to the Gentiles. Paul followed this pattern throughout his missionary days. We see it in action here in verse 1. Usually as he entered a city he went first to the synagog. That, of course, was where he would find the Jewish population centered. But as we noted in the previous chapter, there were also many God-fearing Gentiles who attended the synagog services. That must have been true at **Iconium** because we are told that **a number of both Jews *and Greeks* believed** when he preached in the synagog. And almost as a corresponding pattern we find that when people believed, the unbelieving Jews turned on Paul and used force against him. Here, however, the pattern takes a new twist—the Jews **stirred up the Gentiles** against Paul and Barnabas, **poisoning their minds** against them (v. 2).

This is a natural response of the natural man. When he dislikes what another is doing, he will lash out against him. The first reaction, in many cases, is to **poison the minds** of others. Then you can let them do the dirty work. You will find this response even among Christians in whom there remains much of the old lifestyle. Because many counselees come with bitterness and resentment against others, **poisoning the minds** of people is one of the activities that you should look for in them. In these cases you will be working with believers who have retained one of the most vicious habits that a sinful nature develops—slander. Apart from conversion it probably was not possible to change these Jews. But if your counselee is, as he has professed, a genuine believer, you have at your disposal all the resources necessary to help him to put off this sin. He has the Spirit within, the Scriptures without, and you, representing the church, to assist. That is the biblical combination for change. Instead of responding as these Jews did, counseling affords him the opportunity to "put off" the old ways (cf. Ephesians 4:30, 31) and "put on" God's new ways. Help him to confess his sin to God and to the one he has slandered. Send him to the ones whose minds he has poisoned to confess that he did so in bitterness and malice. Have him ask forgiveness of all concerned. These acts stemming from repentance will be the beginning of a new lifestyle. He must

3   So they spent a considerable amount of time there, boldly speaking for the Lord, Who testified to the message about His grace by doing signs and wonders by their hands.
4   But a large number of the citizens were divided; some were with the Jews, but others were with the apostles.
5   When the Gentiles and the Jews, together with their rulers, made a move to stone them,

---

then start prayerfully practicing putting on kindness and tenderheartedness toward others who may not be all that pleasant to deal with. Having confessed to those concerned, he will not want to go through that experience again, so he should be strongly motivated to learn the new ways of Ephesians 4. But of greater importance, he will realize how greatly he has displeased his Lord and will want to alter his attitudes and behavior mainly for this higher reason.

The apostles **boldly** preached in spite of the opposition (v. 3). Some believed the Jews; others believed Paul and Barnabas. The city was divided (v. 4). But the opposition grew. Finally, there was **a move to stone** the preachers (v. 5) about which they **learned** in time to **escape**. It is clear that **boldness** did not mean foolishness. There was no "macho" thinking on their part. Whenever it became apparent that there was no more that could be done in a town because of the fury of opponents, the preachers knew that they should leave. There were other places to go where they would be received. I have commented on this matter earlier. There is no reason to continue when matters reach that point.

Notice in verse 3 that **the Lord testified to the message about His grace by doing signs and wonders** by the hands of Paul and Barnabas. Here is a plain statement about the purpose of miracles in this period when the church was being established by the work of the apostles. Acts 2:22, I Corinthians 1:6-7, Hebrews 2, and II Corinthians 12:12 also indicate that miracles were for the purpose of authenticating the **message** and the messenger. After all, these men were bringing an inspired message that needed backing. And they were writing inerrant Scripture that needed to be accredited. The **Lord** Jesus used miracles for that purpose (Acts 2:22). Since we are not in that same position today, having received the complete canon of Scripture in which God's full message is inscribed, we no longer need miracles. That is important to explain to those counselees who wrongly may be looking for them.

Next, they traveled into the vicinity of Lystra and Derbe and areas surrounding them preaching (vv. 6, 7). We come to events in **Lystra**, a

6   they learned about it and escaped to Lystra and Derbe, the cities of Lycaonia, and that vicinity,

7   and there they announced the message of good news.

8   Now in Lystra there was sitting a man whose feet were lame. He had been crippled from birth and had never walked.

9   He listened to Paul as he spoke. Paul looked straight at him and saw that he had faith to be healed.

10   He said in a loud voice, "Stand up erect on your feet." And he jumped up and walked.

11   When the crowds saw what Paul did, they shouted in Lycaonian, "The gods have come down to us in human form."

12   Then they called Barnabas "Zeus" and Paul "Hermes" (since he was the principal speaker).

13   The priest of Zeus, whose temple was located at the front of the city, brought bulls and garlands to the city gates to offer sacrifices along with the people.

14   But when the apostles Barnabas and Paul heard this, they ripped their clothes apart and rushed out toward the crowd,

---

place off the beaten trail, where they preached principally to a pagan audience.[1] This was a small, backwoods city populated by what some would call "country bumpkins." It was utterly dependent on rain for water.

The preachers healed a man whose feet had been crippled from birth; he had never walked (vv. 8-10), and when the people saw him jumping and walking they shouted, **"The gods have come down to us in human form!"** And **they called Barnabas "Zeus" and Paul "Hermes."**[2] The reason these two Greek gods are singled out is because of a poem by Ovid in which he used Lystra as the setting for the story about a visit of Jupiter (Zeus) and Mercury (Hermes) to a faithful couple named Baucis and Philemon. The people thought that there was a reappearance of the gods who had supposedly visited their forefathers.

Verse 13 indicates that they were about to offer sacrifices to them in the **temple of Zeus** that was located near the entrance to the city. When the apostles heard this, their natural reaction was a Jewish one—to tear

---

[1] Presumably, there was no synagog there. It took ten Jewish men to constitute one.

[2] Paul, we are told, was **the principal speaker**. That is why he was called Hermes (or Mercury). In Greek and Roman mythology Hermes was the god who brought and explained the messages of the other gods. Hermeneutics, the science of interpretation, derives its name from him.

15 shouting,

> Men, why are you doing this? We too are human beings who have a nature that is just like yours! We are announcing the good news to you to turn from these empty things to a living God, **Who made the sky and the earth and the sea and everything in them**.

16 In past generations He allowed the Gentiles to go their own ways;

17 yet He didn't leave Himself without a witness, since He did good by giving you rain from heaven and fruitful seasons, filling your stomachs with food and your hearts with gladness.

18 So by saying this they barely restrained the crowds from offering a sacrifice to them.

19 But Jews came from Antioch and Iconium and influenced the crowds to stone Paul and drag him outside the city, supposing he was dead.

---

their garments.[1] **They then** proclaimed a message as a result of the event, having first stopped the contemplated sacrifices. Here, the truths of Scripture were proclaimed without appealing to them since the Bible had no authority for pagans. In verses 16 and 17 Paul alludes to the fact that God has been good to them (common grace) in spite of the fact that they have been **going their own ways**. From their explanation, we learn that they **barely restrained the crowds from offering a sacrifice** (v. 18).

Counselees are not likely to mistake you for a god! But in this celebrity-driven society in which we live, counselees that you have helped are very likely to accord you praise and honor that belongs to the Lord. There are those who like to become groupies. You must discourage all such things. Point them to the One Who blessed them. When the atmosphere in counseling is Christ centered from the first session on such misplaced acclaim is not very likely to arise. But, even in spite of your best efforts to give all the credit to your Lord, you will always run into those who want to praise you unduly.

The Jews who had opposed Paul and Barnabas in other cities were so zealous to do them harm that they followed them to Lystra and **influenced the crowds to stone Paul**. They then dragged him out of the city **supposing he was dead** (v. 19). Opposition to truth can at times become quite violent. You will probably not be stoned, but you may be sued. Anyone, it

---

[1] Clothing was expensive and people had few garments which they wore all the time. To tear a garment, then, was no small thing. It was an impressive act that exhibited how greatly one was affected by what was taking place.

20 But when the disciples surrounded him, he got up and entered the city. The next day he left with Barnabas for Derbe.

21 After they announced the good news to that city and made many disciples, they returned to Lystra, Iconium and Antioch,

22 strengthening the lives of the disciples, encouraging them to continue in the faith, and telling them that they must enter God's empire through many afflictions.

23 In every church they appointed elders for them, and with prayer and fasting they committed them to the Lord, in Whom they had believed.

24 They passed through Pisidia and came to Pamphylia.

25 After speaking the Word in Perga, they went down to Attalia,

---

seems, can be sued for almost anything these days. You should keep clear and accurate records. You should be ready to bring in witnesses if possible.[1] Some shy away from counseling for fear of being sued. You cannot let this dissuade you; the day may come when a pastor is even sued for *not* counseling!

Paul was not dead. The disciples **surrounded** him and took him back to Lystra (where, incidentally, he picked up Timothy); he then left the next day for **Derbe**. Some sort of divine enabling, healing or possibly even a resurrection from the dead (as some have thought) was likely. That a person mistaken for dead could travel the next day[2] is hardly likely unless something supernatural had happened to enable him to do so. The **surrounding** of the new converts may indicate a surrounding of him with prayer.

In spite of what had just happened at Lystra (or perhaps **because** of it and the way God provided) the apostles returned to the places where they had preached and had left groups behind in order to **strengthen** and **encourage** the infant churches. They made it clear that **afflictions** were likely to come their way too (vv. 21, 22). There was concern about the outward organization of the church so they appointed elders (cf. v. 23, Titus 1:5). The mission of Paul and Barnabas was no parachurch effort. Converts were not left to fend for themselves.

---

[1] It is wise not to counsel alone if you can help it (never should a man counsel alone with a woman). Always have an elder or trainee present. The value of a witness, as well as the help that another person affords, is worth making the effort.

[2] Especially as travel was carried on in those days (he didn't go by Emergency Medical Service!).

26   and from there they sailed to Antioch, where they had been entrusted to God's grace for the work that they carried out.

27   Upon their arrival they called the church together and reported all that God had done with them, and how He had opened a door of faith to the Gentiles.

28   And they spent a long time with the disciples.

Having left the area, they preached their way back to Antioch **where they had been entrusted to God's grace for the work** by the congregations there. They reported to the church all that God had done and then spent a long time there (vv. 26-28). They recognized their responsibility to their home church. They considered the mission one that reached forth from Antioch. Paul was never a lone wolf. At the same time, he operated with much freedom. That is the ideal combination: make someone responsible, then give him his head. Any man who manifests gifts for ministry ought to be able to operate best under such conditions. The trouble is that we tend to tilt toward one or the other extremes of this middle, biblical course.

CHAPTER 15

1 Now some people came down from Judea who taught the brothers, "Unless you are circumcised according to Moses' custom, you can't be saved."

2   Since this occasioned a good bit of dissension and debate between Paul and Barnabas and these people, they appointed Paul and Barnabas and some others from their number to go up to Jerusalem to talk to the apostles and elders in Jerusalem about this controversy.

The Jerusalem conference described in chapter 15 was convened after Paul's second trip to Jerusalem (mentioned in the book of Galatians).[1] The conference was a critical occasion in the life of the church since it settled once and for all the matter of whether a Gentile had first become a Jew in order to be saved and become a member of the church. The verdict of the council was plain: he did not. What led to the decision on this matter?

Well, doubtless the question had been growing into a controversy ever since Peter's action in Caesarea in the house of Cornelius. And now that the church had been spreading in all directions under the missionary efforts of Paul and Barnabas, and Gentiles were beginning to form a large percentage of the church, it could no longer be avoided. Matters came to a head when some people came down to Antioch from Judea who **taught the brothers** in Antioch that unless they were circumcised they could not **be saved**. This was heresy, the very heresy that Paul had confronted in his letter to the Galatians (v. 1). This was not a peripheral issue. In fact, Paul declared it to be "another gospel" (Galatians 1:6). You can understand then, that the debate was a heated one, just as verse 2 indicates. The word translated **dissension** is used to describe what we would call a *hot* controversy. Because the church was unable to convince the people from Jerusalem, they determined to send Paul, Barnabas and others to **Jerusalem to talk to the apostles and elders** there in order to settle the matter. Accordingly they went, taking time along the way to meet with the churches in Phoenicia and Samara in order to tell them about **the conversion of the Gentiles.** The brothers there rejoiced in hearing of the mission to Cyprus and Asia Minor.

There are always people coming into the church who tend to upset

---

[1] See F.F. Bruce, *Acts* for details.

3   So then the church sent them on their way and they passed through Phoenicia and Samaria, telling the details about the conversion of the Gentiles, and brought great joy to all the brothers.

4 When they arrived in Jerusalem, they received a welcome from the church and the apostles and the elders, and they reported everything that God had done with them.

5   But some believers who had come from the sect of the Pharisees stood up and said, "They must be circumcised and directed to keep Moses' law."

6 The apostles and elders gathered together to see about this matter.

7   After there had been a lot of discussion, Peter got up and said to them, Brothers, you know that at the outset God made a choice among you that the Gentiles should hear and believe the gospel from me.

---

things. This is both bad (they ought not to do so) and good (it gives the true believers an opportunity to better understand and define God's truth for themselves). It would be impossible for a counselor to take up and discuss every doctrinal error that a counselee may hold. But clearly when the doctrine is of such magnitude as this one—the gospel of free grace was at stake—a person must speak up. Counselors must recognize that doctrine leads to life (cf. Titus 1:1). They may not avoid dealing with doctrine by saying, "My work only concerns how a person lives." How he lives will, in the end, be determined by what he believes.[1] All doctrine has consequences for life. All such consequences at root are doctrinal. Avoid doctrine and you avoid life. Astute counselors can trace many life problems back to faulty doctrine.

In verse 4 we read that they were welcomed by the Jerusalem church. Paul and Barnabas then reported about their missionary journey. But some converts from Pharisaism insisted that these new believers must be **circumcised** and keep **Moses' law** (vv. 4, 5). So the **apostles** and the **elders** met to discuss the issue (v. 6). Finally, **Peter** spoke. He reminded the group that God had chosen him to first preach the gospel to the Gentiles (v. 7). And, as he had seen in the house of Cornelius, he also reminded them that God had given Gentile believers the Holy Spirit just as He did to Jews on the day of Pentecost (v. 8). Moreover, this forgiveness and cleansing took place by **faith** alone; God required nothing more. Peter then became personal, putting it to them in these words: "**Why are you testing**

---

[1] If a person thinks you can be saved then lost, for instance, you will spend a lot of time concerning that issue that might otherwise be spent ministering to others. That erroneous doctrine encourages an unbiblical self focus.

8	God, the Heart-knower, testified to them by giving them the Holy Spirit just as He did to us.
9	In no way did He distinguish between us and them when He cleansed their hearts by faith.
10	Now then, why are you testing God by putting on the disciples' neck a yoke that neither our fathers nor we have had the strength to tolerate?
11	Rather, we believe that we will be saved by the grace of the Lord Jesus, in the same way they will.

12 The whole gathering grew silent and listened to Barnabas and Paul relate what signs and wonders God did by them among the Gentiles.

13 When they finished speaking, James replied,

Brothers, listen to me.

God by putting on the disciples' neck a yoke that neither our fathers nor we have had the strength to tolerate."[1] Then he made the great statement that since God in no way distinguished between the Jews and the Gentiles, we must **believe that we will be saved by the grace of the Lord Jesus, in the same way they will** (vv. 9, 11). Nothing could be more explicit. And from the vision that Peter was granted, there was no other conclusion that he could reach.

It is out of concern for truth that discussions and debates take place. It is essential that no real issues be swept under the rug or left unsettled (by leaving the conclusion ambiguous), as so many want to. Clear cut, plain statements of faith are what counselees need to hear from you. Don't fudge. If you don't know an answer, admit it. If you do, don't hedge it. If you need to learn the answer to a counselee's question, tell him you will endeavor to find the answer by the next session. Give him as part of his homework the task of praying that God will enable you to discover the truth of the matter. Then, search it out, if necessary meeting with others to discover God's answer. People need truth. And they need it stated, as Peter did, unequivocally. One of the functions of a counselor, according to Isaiah 41:28, is to provide answers to questions posed to them.

Then the whole gathering grew **quiet** (evidently it had not been till Peter spoke). Paul and Barnabas then told their story of what God had been doing among the Gentiles. Then James, the Lord's brother, spoke. He went back into the Old Testament prophecies that predicted the ingathering of the Gentiles (vv. 12-18) and then concluded by saying, "**my**

---

[1] The law could not be kept. Its purpose was to expose the sinful nature of man.

14   Simon has told us how God at first became concerned about taking a people from the Gentiles to bear His name.

15   The prophets' words agree with this, even as it is written,

16   **After this I will return and rebuild David's fallen tent, and I will rebuild and restore its ruins,**

17   **so that the rest of mankind may seek the Lord, even all the Gentiles who call on My name,**

18   **says the Lord, who accomplishes these things that have been known from ages past.**

19   So then, my judgment is that we shouldn't cause trouble for those Gentiles who turn to God.

20   Instead, we should direct them in writing to abstain from what is polluted by idols, sexual sin, strangled animals and from blood.

21   I say this because for generations Moses has had in every city those who preach him in the synagogs where he is read every Sabbath.

---

judgment is that we shouldn't cause trouble for those Gentiles who turn to God" (v. 19). Instead, he advised that they do nothing more than tell the Gentiles to keep away from those things associated with pagan worship (v. 20), for the sake of winning the Jews among them (v. 21).

There was good judgment behind these words. It was not an absolute command that the Gentiles refrain from these things (except, of course fornication[1]). But they thought it would be wise in attempting to witness to the Jews in their communities. These would be the things that would offer the greatest offense. The group gathered agreed with James that this was a fine solution, and they chose some trusted men to accompany the delegation that was returning to Antioch to bring the message officially to them.

This conference indicates that the congregations were not independent (this is clear especially when you read 16:4 where the churches are told to **obey** the decisions of the Jerusalem council). And this council also indicates that churches should settle matters of doctrinal controversy in conference from the Scriptures. Moreover, it shows how leaders in the church are to be heard and their views respected. There is much here to relate to counselees who want to thrust aside all church authority.

So the council composed a letter (vv. 23-29) to the church at Antioch indicating the following events: 1) to upset the church there some mem-

---

[1] Prostitution was considered an acceptable part of the temple worship among many Gentiles.

22 Then it seemed good to the apostles, the elders and the whole church to choose some of their men to send to Antioch with Paul and Barnabas—Judas, called Barsabbas, and Silas, leading men among the brothers.

23 This is the letter they sent by them:

> The apostles and the brothers who are elders to the Gentile brothers in Antioch, Syria and Cilicia: Greetings.
>
> 24 Because we heard that some of our members, without our authorization, have caused you trouble by what they said, unsettling your minds,
>
> 25 it seemed good to us, upon unanimous agreement, to choose men and send them to you with our dear friends Barnabas and Paul,
>
> 26 men who have risked their lives for the sake of the Name of our Lord Jesus Christ.
>
> 27 So we sent Judas and Silas, who by word of mouth will tell you the same things.
>
> 28 It seemed good to the Holy Spirit and to us not to lay any additional burden on you than these essentials:
>
> 29 abstain from idol sacrifices, from blood, from strangled animals and from sexual sin. If you keep yourselves from these things, you will do well. Farewell.

30 Then they were sent off and went down to Antioch, and when they had gathered the group together, they delivered the letter.

31 When they read it, they rejoiced at its encouragement.

---

bers stirred up trouble **without their authorization**[1] (v. 24;); 2) **there was unanimous agreement**[2] about the outcome of their discussion; 3) they were sending men with Paul and Barnabas, whose courageous work they commended, to explain everything to them; 4) neither they nor the Spirit's message through the Bible indicated that any other **burden** should be laid on the Gentiles except that they avoid temple worship with all its pitfalls. They returned to Antioch, **gathered** the church together, and **delivered the letter**. The church **rejoiced** at the encouraging words they heard (vv. 30, 31). And the **prophets Judas and Silas**, who had come from Jerusalem, were of great help by means of their words. Finally, the church at Antioch paid their way back to Jerusalem.

---

[1] Consider the implications of that phrase with respect to church authority!

[2] Not all debates will end in such agreement (cf. II Corinthians 2:6). Those churches that will not take an action apart from unanimity err. They thereby set up *minority* rule in the church!

32 And Judas and Silas, who themselves were prophets, encouraged and strengthened the brothers by the many things that they said.

33 After spending some time there, the brothers sent them back with peace to those who sent them.

34 ¹

35 But Paul and Barnabas stayed in Antioch, teaching and announcing the Lord's message of good news with many others also.

36 After some days Paul said to Barnabas,

Let us return and look in on the brothers in every city in which we preached the Lord's Word, and see how they are.

37 Barnabas wanted to take John, who was called Mark, with them.

38 But Paul didn't think it would be right to take him, since he had deserted them in Pamphylia and hadn't gone on with them in the work.

---

¹ Some MSS add vs. 34: *But it seemed good to Silas to stay there.*

It was important for the church at Jerusalem to treat this matter seriously and to take all these precautions of sending men to Antioch (at considerable expense, you can be sure for a church that itself was impoverished). Matters of consequence—as this was—need to be treated with all the concern that they merit. Too often in the church financial considerations determine our actions rather than other more important factors. Teach counselees the proper attitude toward these things.

In time, Paul and Barnabas became concerned about how their new converts along the Northwestern Mediterranean rim were doing. They determined to go and find out (v. 36). But a problem arose. **Barnabas**, ever the encourager, wanted to take John **Mark** who had **deserted them** in Pamphylia (presumably when the going got tough). Paul pointed this out and disagreed. The two men could not reconcile their different views; because of **sharp disagreement over the matter**, eventually they went separate ways, Barnabas and Mark to Cyprus and Paul and Silas to Syria and Cilicia. There are times when brothers must simply agree to disagree.¹ They should not disagree over essential doctrine nor censurable offenses, but over matters of judgment as this was. Counselees are not always too clear about such distinctions. You must be clear in order to

---

¹ Paul eventually agreed that Mark's services had become profitable (II Timothy 4:11, Paul's last letter). Was he concerned to set this matter to rest after all these years?

39 There arose such a sharp disagreement that they separated from one
another. Barnabas took Mark and sailed off for Cyprus,
40 but Paul chose Silas and went off, commended to the Lord's grace by
the brothers.
41 And he went through Syria and Cilicia, strengthening the churches.

---

advise them well. A matter of judgment (what might be best) is not the
same as a matter of doctrinal or moral purity. It is heartening to see the
doctrinal issue resolved by the Jerusalem council. It is not so heartening to
see that the judgment issue could not be.

CHAPTER 16

1 Now he also came down to Derbe and to Lystra. And there was a certain disciple there named Timothy, who was the son of a believing Jewess, and his father was a Greek.
2 He was well spoken of by the brothers in Lystra and Iconium.

At this point Barnabas drops out of the picture and in the remainder of the book of Acts we take up the missionary journeys of Paul and his various companions. In God's providence it was crucial for the separation of Paul and Barnabas. Paul, in charge and with more dependable assistants, did what he, Barnabas and Mark might never had. In God's world even sad occurrences (like their separation) are used for His glory and the promotion and welfare of His church. Counselees must be given a broader perspective than the one that they so often bring into the counseling room. Many see no further than the immediate problem that is plaguing them. They must be taught to consider it not only in the light of eternity in which all wrongs will be righted, but also in the near future when they may begin to learn something of how God turns evil into good. That is what we see here. Mark's defection and the subsequent argument between Paul and Barnabas led to the mission of Paul that ultimately took the gospel to Rome. Since this mission was outlined in Acts 1:8, it is clear that God had providentially planned the event. God does not merely plan ends; He also plans the means that lead to those ends. If we believe Romans 8:28, we will also believe that He can bring righteous outcomes even from man's sinful activities. This understanding helps counselees to view happenings in their lives differently. Help them to understand that they live within the realm of God's providence. One thing that should be immediately discernible is that difficulties happen to help shape us into Christ's image (cf. Romans 8:28, 29).

Timothy, who had become a believer on the first trip to Lystra, took the place of Mark as Paul's faithful companion. Timothy would be true to the end (Paul's last letter, remember, was to Timothy[1]). It is interesting that following the Jerusalem council and after writing the letter to the Galatians, Paul was sensitive enough to the bias of the Jews that he had

---

[1] In II Timothy, Paul hands over his ministry to Timothy to take up where he would leave off.

3   Paul wanted him to go along with him, so he circumcised him because of the Jews who were in those areas, since they knew that his father was a Greek.

4   As they traveled through these cities, they delivered the decisions reached by the apostles and the elders at Jerusalem, and told them to obey them.

5   So the churches were strengthened in the faith and grew in numbers daily.

6 They went through the country of Phrygia and Galatia, having been prevented by the Holy Spirit from speaking the Word in Asia.

7   As they went toward Mysia, they attempted to enter Bithynia, but the Spirit of Jesus wouldn't let them.

8   So they passed by Mysia and went down to Troas.

Timothy circumcised (v. 3). In that way, problems would be averted in preaching in the synagogs. While on one hand Paul would fight tooth and nail to see that the clarity of the gospel was not compromised, on the other hand he would not let (what had now become) a cultural difference get in the way of proclaiming it. Juxtaposed against the discussion in the last chapter, Paul's action demonstrates not inconsistency but wisdom. Here is a man who could distinguish between circumcision as a way to salvation and circumcision as the way in which one is able to get a hearing among the Jews. That same sort of distinction is one that many of your counselees may fail to make about various issues. There is a place where one cannot compromise; there is also a place where it is wise to do so. Christian liberty must be asserted against those Christians who would take it away; but Christian liberty should be relinquished when it gets in the way of witnessing to unbelievers.

As Paul and his companions traveled, they took the letter from the Jerusalem council to each of the churches that they visited (v. 4). Notice that they told the members of these churches to **obey** the injunctions given. Again, while the Jerusalem injunctions were authoritative, they were not to be considered essential to salvation. Exactly not that! They were instead ways in which those who were saved were to live in communities where they were trying to win Jews to the faith (cf. 15:21). Presumably, the churches were doing quite well in these pristine days of the faith. Believers were becoming strong in the faith, and many unbelievers were being converted (v. 5).

The **Holy Spirit**, in ways that we are not told (perhaps through prophetic revelation), guided them rather closely as to where they should

103

9   During the night Paul had a vision of a Macedonian man standing there urging him in these words, "Come over to Macedonia and help us."

10 So when he saw the vision, at once we tried to go into Macedonia, concluding that God had called us to announce the message of good news to them.

11 Setting sail from Troas, we ran a straight course to Samothrace, the next day went on to Neapolis,

12 and from there to Philippi, which is a colony and the leading city of that part of Macedonia. And we stayed in this city for a number of days.

13 On the Sabbath we went outside the gate to a place by a river, where we expected to find a place of prayer. We sat down and spoke to the women who had gathered there.

14 A woman named Lydia, from the city of Thyatira, who sold purple goods and was a worshiper of God, heard, and the Lord opened her heart to pay attention to what Paul said.

15 When she and her household were baptized, she urged us this way: "If you have determined that I am faithful to the Lord, come and stay at my house." And she prevailed upon us to do so.

---

preach (vv. 6-8) We are allowed to see, however, that it was through a **vision** that Paul entered **Macedonia** (v. 9). Here was new territory. Paul had set out to visit the brothers in the newly founded churches (15:36, 41), but the journey turned into something else. God has a way of opening new horizons for those who pursue responsibilities faithfully. If they are faithful in small things, He opens larger ones for them. Here is a truth to inculcate.

So Paul understood and obeyed the vision (vv. 10, 11), and ended up in Philippi where he had a very successful ministry (v. 12). Evidently there was no synagog, so Paul looked for a prayer place where Jews would assemble in lieu of a synagog. Finding it along side the river, he discovered several women gathered there. He spoke to them about Christ, and Lydia, a seller of purple garments who was from Thyatira, believed. She and her entire household were baptized. She invited Paul and his company to stay in her house while in the city (vv. 13-15). This was the beginning of a brand new ministry to Europe.

True conversion leads to works. There wasn't much that this new convert could do since she knew so little, but there were some things. She, a woman of means, could provide room and board for the missionary team. She could introduce her household to the new faith. She could listen and learn from those who lived in her house. There are always things that any and every convert can do to further the faith—even from the begin-

16 Now it so happened that as we were going to the place of prayer a slave girl with a divining spirit, whose fortune-telling brought her owners a lot of money, met us.

17 She followed Paul and us, shouting, "These people are the Most High God's slaves, who announce the way of salvation to you."

18 She did this for a number of days. But Paul became so annoyed that he turned around and said to the spirit, "In the name of Jesus Christ I order you to leave her!" And it left her at that very hour.

19 Now when her owners saw that their way of making money for the future was gone, they grabbed Paul and Silas and dragged them to the marketplace to the rulers.

20 When they had brought them before the chief magistrates, they said, "These persons are Jews and are causing our city a lot of trouble.

21 They are advocating customs that it isn't lawful for us Romans to receive or practice."

22 The crowd joined in attacking them, and the magistrates tore off their clothes and ordered them to be beaten.

23 After many stripes had been laid on them, they threw them into prison, ordering the jailer to keep them securely.

---

ning of their new life. Many counselees who are confronted with their failure to do works that are appropriate to salvation could learn from the example of Lydia. Some keep on waiting till they are "ready."

At Philippi, the team met a **slave girl** who was a **fortune teller** and who **brought her owners a lot of money**. The demon who was in her was the source of her ability to tell fortunes (doubtless through deception and fraud). But because of the coming defeat of the Satanic world at the cross (Colossians 2), for some reason unknown to us, the demon seemed compelled to acknowledge and announce through her that the preachers had come from God to teach the way of **salvation** (vv. 16-17). She followed Paul and his team **shouting** this fact for days on end. Paul became **annoyed** at this and exorcised the unclean spirit. The owners became furious, since this took away her ability to tell fortunes and, consequently, their sordid livelihood. They grabbed Paul and Silas and brought them to the town square before the rulers (vv. 17-19). They told the rulers that Jews had appeared, were causing trouble in the city, and were teaching beliefs un**lawful for Romans to receive or practice**. Notice that they omitted the true reason for their concern—money! Again and again you and your counselees will encounter this sort of thing. People will make accusations that have some basis in fact as the reason for their opposition,

24 So when he received this sort of charge, he threw them into the inner prison and secured their feet in the stocks.

25 But about midnight Paul and Silas were praying and singing hymns to God, and the prisoners were listening to them,

26 when suddenly the ground shook so violently that the jail's foundations quivered, and all at once all the doors swung open and all the chains fell apart.

27 When the jailer awakened, he saw that the doors of the prison were open and had drawn his sword and was about to kill himself, because he thought the prisoners had escaped.

28 But Paul shouted out, "Don't harm yourself! We're all here!"

29 He asked for lights, rushed in and, trembling with fear, he fell before Paul and Silas.

30 Then he led them out and said, "Sirs, what must I do to be saved?"

31 They said, "Believe on the Lord Jesus and you will be saved, you and your household."

---

but they will omit the real motive behind it. This is a trait of sinful human nature: distort the facts (sometimes only by omission) in order to make the case. No one should be surprised when this happens to him. But counselors should become astute enough to penetrate subterfuges. They should learn the truth about such things by unearthing all the facts.

On the grounds of insufficient evidence, they were beaten and imprisoned. The jailer was told to **keep them securely**, so he threw them into the **inner prison**, the most secure place of all. But at midnight, Paul and Silas were **singing hymns and praying**. The prisoners **were listening to them**, doubtless in astonishment. Suddenly, there was an **earthquake**, the **doors** of the prison opened, and the **chains** fell apart. The jailer awakened, saw the open doors, and supposed that his prisoners had escaped. He was about to kill himself with his **sword** when Paul spoke and said, "**Don't harm yourself! We're all here!**" The jailer rushed in, and in the face of death and this extraordinary happening fell trembling before Paul and Silas. Then, leading them out of the inner prison he said, "**What must I do to be saved?**" Their great response was, "**Believe on the Lord Jesus and you will be saved, you and your household.**" Probably the jailer had heard something of the witness of the team members, and perhaps even had been impressed with their demeanor and their singing. But, whatever the facts were, he recognized in these men that there was something different that he needed. So he asked how he could be **saved**. The clear answer was given—have faith in Christ.

32 So they told him God's message, along with those who were in his household.

33 He took them in that very hour of the night and washed their stripes, and he and all his family were baptized right away.

34 Then he brought them to his house and made a meal for them and, together with his whole household, rejoiced that he had believed in God.

Difficulty, persecution, injury—all of these things—are opportunities for furthering the faith. But the way in which a person handles these may make all the difference. If, like the team in Philippi, he handles trouble with singing (literally or figuratively), he may have a significant witness for Christ. If he complains, whines, gets angry, and such, he will probably forfeit any such witness. Tell that to suffering counselees—especially to those who suffer unjustly. That is a powerful way to teach that lesson. After all, why not sing? It is all in God's providence, isn't it? Things are not beyond His control. Indeed, He is at work in one way or another furthering His church. Get that into the heads of counselees who can see nothing beyond their sore backs. Paul and Silas are great examples of how God expects us to live through persecution for Him.

They explained the message to the jailer and his household, he washed their stripes, and the jailer and his family were baptized into the church right away. Notice, Paul did not wait until morning to bring him into the church. Even with a bloody back, at midnight, he baptized the family into church membership. We are sometimes loath to bring people in, holding them off too long. On the other hand, many are hesitant to join. All of this needs to change. We should not require prospective members to attend courses several weeks (months) long before they are admitted into the church. Here, with the Ethiopian eunuch and with the multitudes on Pentecost and following, we see people admitted into membership on the spot. We need to do the same today. The courses can come later. People who complete a membership course think they have graduated from learning. People who are admitted right away should be told that they are admitted into Christ's school and will be expected to learn all their lives.[1] They graduate into heaven! One major reason we fail to do as we should in this matter is because we have abandoned church discipline. We make it (a little) hard to get into the church, but once in, the person is in for good, no matter what he does. So we want to be sure beforehand.

---

[1] Note the order in Matthew 28:18-20: first admission by baptism, *then* teaching.

35 When daylight came, the magistrates sent their officers, saying, "Let those men go."

36 The jailer reported these words to Paul: "The magistrates have sent them to release you. Now then, come out and go in peace."

37 But Paul said to them,

> They beat us publicly without a trial, even though we are Romans; and they threw us into prison. Now are they going to get rid of us secretly? No indeed! Rather, let them come themselves and bring us out!

38 So the officers reported these words to the magistrates, and they were afraid when they heard that they were Romans.

39 So they came and apologized to them and brought them out and asked them to leave the city.

40 Then they left the prison and entered Lydia's house, and when they had seen the brothers, they encouraged them and left.

You really can't be. It should be easy to get into the church, but it should be more difficult to remain. That is to say, one should realize that he may be put out of the church if and when he becomes unwilling to hear the authority of Jesus Christ vested in the church (Matthew 18:15ff.). That way membership means something. Where there is no church discipline, membership is cheapened.

At daylight, the magistrates, who presumably had had time to investigate the matter, told the jailer to let Paul and Silas go free. But Paul said no. Since they had been beaten publicly, even though they were Romans (something that was unlawful), Paul insisted that the magistrates themselves come and bring them out. The magistrates acquiesced when they realized that they had unlawfully beaten Roman citizens. They came, apologized, and asked them to leave the city.[1] The preachers went back to Lydia's house, encouraged the believers who had gathered there, and left. What a powerful chapter! God is at work providentially. This needs to be heralded by counselors far and wide.

---

[1] Throughout Acts we see Paul standing up for his rights as a Roman citizen.

CHAPTER 17

1 Now when they had gone through Amphipolis and Apollonia, they came to Thessalonica, where there was a Jewish synagog.

2   So, according to his custom, Paul went to their meeting and for three Sabbaths he reasoned with them from the Scriptures,

---

It is about 100 miles from Philippi to Thessalonica. Having traveled that distance, the preaching team arrived and began ministering, **according to custom**, at the local synagog. There, for three weeks, **Paul reasoned** with the Jews about the truth of Christianity (v. 2). There are those who have a very different attitude about how ministry should be carried on. They see no need for reasoning with anyone.[1] They piously say things like, "God's Word needs no defense. I simply present the truth and leave it there. Reasoning gets the human element into the presentation. It is God who must save." Such arguments hold not a thimble's worth of water. The apostle Paul reasoned. If he saw the need for doing so, then you and I should also see the need. The human element is precisely what a preacher or counselor brings to the presentation. God did not choose to write His message in the sky. It was the foolishness of preaching (human exposition and presentation of the message) that, for His own purposes, God chose to use in bringing people to Christ. Of course *God* saves, but He uses human personality to deliver the saving message to the lost. Counseling is person to person ministry. There is an element that is essential in this personal ministry that we may never bypass, and that is reasoning. Any counselor who fails to reason in counseling is doing something other than biblical counseling.[2]

But it is not bare reasoning that Paul did—or that you should do. Paul reasoned **from the Scriptures.** That is the key to it all. Those who reason as Paul did do not reason from their experiences, from human ideas, or even from general revelation. In order to bring about salvation or sanctification they reason from the **Scriptures.** Later in the chapter we shall see Paul speaking to Gentiles. He cannot use the Bible as an author-

---

[1] One cannot help wondering whether they shy off because they do not know how to reason. Some, perhaps, simply don't like the give-and-take of debate and discussion.

[2] Rogerians, for instance, do not reason. There is nothing reasonable about what they do.

109

3   opening up and setting forth for them the fact that the Christ had to suffer and to rise again from the dead, and that "this Jesus Whom I am announcing to you is the Christ."

4   Some of them were persuaded and threw in their lot with Paul and Silas, as did a large number of the God-fearing Greeks, along with a number of the most prominent women.

---

ity with them, but he can certainly teach the truths that have been revealed in it; this is exactly what he does. Reasoning and persuading people from the Scriptures overtly and covertly is the standard practice of the biblical counselor when he meets with those who seek help from God (cf. Acts 28:23). There is nothing worthwhile that I have to offer others that has not first been given by God. My ministry would be over the instant I was told that I must reason with men and women from my own thoughts and ideas. Though the human element is necessary, the human element is not the source of the content that is presented. Biblical truths are presented by a human counselor to human beings through reasoning that helps them understand and appropriate what God has revealed.

How did Paul do it? Like His Lord on the road to Emmaus (Luke 24:32), he **opened up** the Scriptures to the listener. This **opening** means that he so explained the meaning of the passages to which he referred that the listener could see for himself what God was saying in them. Thus, all the authority for what he said came from God—not from himself.[1] Every biblical counselor must so thoroughly understand the Bible passages that he uses and must so clearly **set them forth** that, when he has completed his exposition, the counselee knows that God in the Bible has said what he has set forth. Here, of course, Paul presented the gospel to these people from the Old Testament. In this presentation of truth then, as in all that is properly presented from the Bible, there was exegesis, exposition, argument, persuasion and application (vv. 2, 3). If you don't know the meaning of these terms, or don't know how to accomplish any or all of them, you need to acquire the prerequisite knowledge and skills. The counselor must do the very things that a good preacher does.

Some **Jews** and a large number of the **God-fearing Gentiles** came to faith in Christ. It is interesting that a **number of the most prominent women** is mentioned (v. 4). Women have always been a large part of the

---

[1] Scripture unopened is often not understood, thus obliging the listener to take what the counselor says as true simply because *he* says so. When it is opened, he sees *for himself* that *God, not merely the counselor,* is saying it.

5   But the Jews were jealous and gathered up some of the worthless rabble that lounged around the marketplace; they formed a mob and began to cause trouble in the city. They crowded around Jason's house looking for them, so they could bring them out to the mob.

6   But when they couldn't find them they dragged Jason and some of the brothers before the civil authorities, shouting,

> These persons who have turned the world upside down have come here too,

7   and Jason has welcomed them! They are all acting contrary to Caesar's decrees, saying that there is a different emperor—Jesus!

8   The crowd and the authorities were disturbed when they heard this,

9   and they released Jason and the rest only on bail.

   10   Then the brothers at once sent Paul and Silas away by night to Berea. When they arrived, they went into the Jewish synagog.

11   Now these Jews were more noble than those in Thessalonica, and they received the Word with great eagerness, examining the Scriptures daily to see if these things were so.

---

church of Christ. Evidently, because the women were of influence, they were able to lend strong support to the missionary effort. But in spite of the generally good reception and the founding of a church, the Jews as a whole **zealously** opposed what was happening. They **gathered up some of the worthless rabble that lounged around the marketplace** and induced them to cause trouble for the preaching team. This **mob** gathered around the house where they had been lodging. But for some reason, they couldn't find them. So they dragged out **Jason**, who owned the house, and brought him before the **civil authorities**. They represented the apostles as those who had been causing trouble everywhere and who were saying things about a new emperor—Jesus. This of course, had it been true in the sense in which it was presented, would have been treason (v. 6). There was concern expressed, and Jason was released only on bail (vv. 8, 9).

Because of the violence of the opposition, the **brothers** packed **Paul and Silas off by night to Berea.** Upon arrival, they wasted no time attending the synagog service, where as usual they preached Christ (vv. 10, 11). The Jews in Berea, unlike those to whom they had ministered to previously, **were more noble** and received the Word of God with **great eagerness**. What made the difference? Here, in Berea, they **examined the Scriptures daily to see if these things were so** (v. 11). If one thing is plain throughout the Bible it is that those who submit themselves to the Scriptures not only come to know the truth, but also rejoice in it and seek

12 As a result, many of them believed, and also many Greek women of high standing, and a number of Greek men.

13 But when the Jews from Thessalonica learned that God's Word had been announced by Paul in Berea also, they went there also to agitate and stir up the crowds.

14 So the brothers sent Paul off at once as far as the sea, but Silas and Timothy stayed there.

15 Those who accompanied Paul brought him as far as Athens, and took back an order to Silas and Timothy that they should come as soon as possible.

16 Now while Paul was waiting for them at Athens, he was enraged within as he looked at the city filled with images.

17 So he reasoned in the synagog with the Jews and the God-fearing Greeks, and every day in the marketplace with those who happened to be there.

---

to live for God as they should. What made the difference was their willingness not to prejudge or allow envy to cloud their judgment, but to find out the truth. These men were truth seekers. Truth seeking counselees are a joy to counsel. They do not make excuses, they are willing to hear the truth even when it hurts, and they will align themselves with it over against every and anything else. Because they searched the Scriptures, we are told that **many** Bereans **believed** (v. 12). There was an influx of **Greeks** as well.

The Jews at Thessalonica were so zealous to stamp out the new faith that they traveled to Berea and stirred up trouble among the crowds. Again the brothers sent Paul off as far as **Athens**, though the others remained.[1] Paul, through a letter, urged Timothy and Silas to come as soon as possible. Paul toured the city of Athens while he waited for them. But he was no tourist. Indeed, rather than remarking about the "fine architecture and wonderful works of art" as he looked at the idolatry represented on every hand, we read that **he was enraged within** (v. 16). It struck him that here—in the supposed intellectual center of the world— were **images** of false gods everywhere he **looked**. There was a proverb in the air at the time that said "In Athens it is easier to find a god than a man." We are told that there were more statues in Athens than in all of the

---

[1] Paul's being spirited out of the towns by the brothers was probably due to his weakened condition after the beating at Philippi. It certainly had nothing to do with cowardice.

18 Then some of the Epicurean and Stoic philosophers took him on. Some said, "What does this eclectic babbler want to say?" And others, "He seems to be promoting some foreign gods." (They said this because he announced the good news about Jesus and the resurrection.)

---

other Greek cities put together.

Paul went to the **synagog** where he reasoned with the Jews and the God-fearers. But every day he also went to the marketplace to speak with those he could find there.[1] As he presented the gospel to those who assembled, **some Epicureans and Stoics took him on**. They called him an **eclectic babbler**.[2] It is important to understand something about both of these philosophical sects if you want to understand Paul's speech before the Areopagus. **The Stoics** were a group founded by Zeno.[3] They believed that a person must live in conformity to nature. One must convince himself that whatever happens is good and right and must go with the flow. Their god was identified with matter (Stoics were pantheists). They were uncertain about future life. Apathy (never to become too happy nor too sad about anything; strike a happy medium) was the goal. Epictitus, the lame slave, was their most famous teacher.[4] The view might be summed up as follows: pleasure is no good; pain is no evil.

Epicureans were rivals of the Stoics. They were founded by Epicurus who lived a life apart. He taught in a garden, wrote 300 books[5] and lived on beans, bread and water. They were atheists. The gods, they held, were but phantoms of people's minds. They sought, but could not find, a canon (a standard by which to measure all things[6]). They were materialists who believed that matter was the only reality. Like modern behaviorists, they thought the mind was purely material. They did believe in

---

[1] The marketplace was roughly equivalent to our modern mall.

[2] The word of opprobrium used here means, literally, "a seed-picker of words." The picture is of a bird picking up a seed here and there as he bounces from place to place. They thought of Paul as someone who had picked up ideas here and there and put them together in an eclectic mishmash. Soon, they were to find out otherwise.

[3] Cleanthes, whom Paul will quote to turn their own guns on themselves, was a cofounder.

[4] His writings are available in the *Loeb Classical Library*.

[5] All of which have perished.

[6] Ignorant of the fact that God gave a revelation for that very purpose.

19 So they took him and led him before the council of the Areopagus, saying,

> Can you tell us about this new teaching of which you have been speaking?

20 You have been bringing some startling information to our ears. So we want to know just what this means.

21 (Now all the Athenians and the foreigners who lived there spent their time doing nothing else but discussing and listening to new ideas.)

---

chance, but denied the future life and any sort of resurrection or immortality. To put their beliefs in the form of a slogan, they said, "pleasure is good, pain is evil." There were two sorts of Epicureans: those who sought pleasure in sordid ways, and those who realized that these ways ultimately brought only pain and so refrained from them.

All of these beliefs, in one form or another, are abroad in our culture today. Your counselees are influenced by them. You must know how to deal with them. Paul's address deals with the lot. It is a very valuable source from which to glean answers and responses to such beliefs whenever they surface in counseling.

Note in verse 19 that Paul was taken to the council of the Areopagus. One reason for this was because he had been setting forth **new teaching**. The Areopagus determined and licensed the religions that it was permissible to follow in Athens. So the speech in a sense was a hearing, but not a trial. This very body, years before, had condemned Socrates for corrupting the youth and setting forth new religious teaching.[1] One of these two charges was now being leveled against Paul. This was serious business; Socrates had been required by the Areopagus to drink the fatal hemlock. Here was Paul, alone before this august body, for a hearing about his **new teaching**. There was a possibility that he too might be condemned.

An interesting comment is made by Luke about the Athenians. He explains that they spent their time discussing new ideas. It was okay to discuss most anything theoretically; it was another thing to set forth a new religion. So while they wanted to hear the **startling information** that Paul had to present, they also recognized that this should be done in the presence of the religion-licensing board. How did Paul slip out of the noose that they were placing over his head?

He began his speech with his observations about the city. Seeming to commend them, he says, "**Men of Athens, everything I see shows me**

---

[1] Socrates taught that he was possessed by a guiding daemon that dwelled within him.

22 Then Paul stood up in the midst of the council of the Areopagus and said,

Men of Athens, everything I see shows me how very religious you are.

23 For example, as I was passing along, looking at your objects of worship, I even found an altar with this inscription: TO AN UNKNOWN GOD. So then, what you worship in ignorance is that which I am announcing to you!

24 The God Who made the world and everything in it, Who is the Lord of heaven and earth, doesn't live in temples made by human hands.

25 Nor is He served by human hands as though He needed something, since He Himself gives life and breath to everybody and everything.

26 He made from one person every human nation to live on the face of the whole earth, and He determined the periods of their exis-

---

how very religious you are." The Athenians, doubtless, were pleased with this, but recognized that Paul might simply be buttering them up. But he was neither commending nor flattering them. Nor was he seeking rapport as many have thought. No, he was grasping the noose and getting ready to take it from his neck and place it on theirs!

He gave an example to support his thesis: "**as I was passing along, looking at your objects of worship, I even found an altar with this inscription: TO AN UNKNOWN GOD.**" They had hoped to cover all bases by erecting this altar. After all, there were so many gods and goddesses they might have forgotten one! But Paul uses this inscription to his advantage. He has slipped them within the noose. He now pulls the rope: "**So then, what you worship in ignorance is that which I am announcing to you!**" He could not be charged with setting forth a new religion. He was simply announcing the religion about which they were ignorant!

There must have been enough astute thinkers in the crowd to understand that they had been had. I am sure that there were some who must have smiled and said, "Well, I guess he got us there." It is important to learn how to turn a situation that seems dangerous (as this was) to one's advantage. As a counselor, you should learn to use something in the counseling milieu to make your point—or to get a hearing. Having disposed of the dangerous charge, Paul then proceeded to challenge with Christian doctrine every one of the Stoic and Epicurean beliefs that I set forth above. I shall not go through the speech verse by verse. Rather, let me outline it:

27   tence and boundaries within which they would live,
27   so that they might seek God, if only they would grope their way to Him and find Him (though He isn't far from any one of us).
28   This is true since
         "In Him we live and move and exist."
         As some of your poets have said,
         "For we also are His family."
29   So, if we are God's family, we ought not think that the Deity resembles gold or silver or stone, or anything engraved by human imagination and skill.
30   God overlooked the times of ignorance, but now He declares that every human being everywhere must repent,
31   because He has set a day in which He is going to judge the world with justice by a Man Whom He has designated to do so. And He has furnished proof of this to everybody by raising Him from the dead.

32 Now when they heard of the resurrection from the dead, some scoffed, but others said, "We want to hear you speak about this again."

33 So Paul left them.

34 But some men joined him and believed, among whom was Dionysius the Areopagite and a woman named Damaris, and others with them.

Introduction: I see you don't know the God I preach;
              let me introduce you to Him.
    I.   He created and sustains you (vv. 24, 25).
   II.   He cannot be represented by idols (v. 29).
  III.   He sent His Son to die for sinners like you (vv. 29-31).
Conclusion: Repent and believe the gospel.

The results of this impromptu speech were phenomenal. Quite contrary to the idea that it was a failure[1] (as some maintain), there were remarkable results. Suppose you gave one unprepared talk at Harvard and at the conclusion you had a trustee, a prominent teacher, a handful of students, and others who wanted to hear more. Wouldn't you consider that a pretty good day's work? I think you would. Here, at the Harvard of the ancient world, Paul accomplished just that. It is true that some **scoffed** when they heard about the resurrection, but wouldn't you expect scoffers at Harvard?

---

[1] It couldn't have been since it was Spirit inspired (see ch. 2). I Corinthians 1-2 which is used to bolster this erroneous interpretation, does not teach that Paul changed his approach (a misunderstanding of I Corinthians). Paul is making it clear that he divorces himself from the tricks of the Sophists. He *always* did. He wants people to believe because they understand what the Spirit has revealed.

CHAPTER 18

1 After this he left Athens and went to Corinth.

2 And he found a certain Jew, named Aquila, a native of Pontus who recently had come from Italy with his wife Priscilla because Claudius had ordered all the Jews to leave Rome. He went to see them.

3 Because they were tentmakers and he worked at the same trade, he stayed with them and worked with them.

4 And every Sabbath in the synagog he reasoned with both the Jews and the Greeks.

5 But by the time that Silas and Timothy came down from Macedonia, Paul was devoting his efforts exclusively to preaching, testifying to the Jews that Jesus was the Christ.

Leaving **Athens**, Paul traveled to **Corinth** (v. 1). Here, Paul contracted to work with **Aquila**, a fellow **tentmaker**. Aquila and his wife Priscilla either were converts before or became so while working with Paul. Probably they were converted under Paul's ministry because when Aquila is first mentioned (v. 2), he is called a **Jew** and not a **brother**. Counselees working with unbelievers should be instructed to bear a good witness to them both by life and by words. Doubtless Paul was a careful worker as well as a good and faithful witness. When the two match they make a powerful impact for Christ.

Again, on the Sabbaths, being free from work, Paul went to the synagog **where he reasoned with both the Jews and the Greeks**. But by the time that Timothy and Silas returned from Macedonia, Paul was **devoting his efforts exclusively to preaching**. That is what he *wanted* to do, of course. But he was not too proud to work at manual labor when necessary. There are dilettante counselors who would never think of stooping to do anything that might get their hands dirty. Such persons will rarely become good counselors. They will know about problems from books, but they will know little about people and their problems from workaday experience. Both are necessary. Doubtless Paul was a better preacher and counselor because he worked at tentmaking.

But once more the Jews (as a whole) **opposed and blasphemed him** (v. 6). As in the past, Paul then turned to the Gentiles. But not before saying to them, "**Your blood be on your heads. I am clean.**" He had been the faithful watchman on the tower. He had sounded the alarm and shown the way of escape. If they refused to hear, he was not responsible; they

117

6   But when they opposed and blasphemed him, he shook out his clothes and said to them, "Your blood be on your heads. I am clean. From now on I am going to the Gentiles!"

7   So he left there and went to the house of a person named Titus Justus, a God-fearing Greek, whose house was next door to the synagog.

8 Now Crispus, the synagog ruler, believed the Lord, together with his whole household, and many of the Corinthians who heard believed and were baptized.

---

would have no one to blame but themselves. There is a time when all has been done, discipline has been followed, and the counselee has been put out of the church. At this point the counselor should also throw in the towel. He no longer should counsel, but should evangelize. The counselee must be treated as these Jews were by Paul—as a heathen and publican.

Paul left the synagog and moved **next door to the house of Titus Justus, a God-fearer** (v. 7). But Paul was not altogether unsuccessful. There were the God-fearing Greeks who believed, there was Titus Justus and there were Aquila and Priscilla. He also was able to introduce Crispus, the ruler of the synagog, to Christ (v. 8). And there were many other Corinthians who believed.

In God's good providence, discouragement on the one hand is often balanced by encouragement on the other hand. The **fear** of failure, however, can powerfully inhibit the work for the Lord. For some reason there must have been a bit of this in the heart of Paul at this time. Again and again he had been turned down by the Jews. Again and again, they had hounded him, even following him to distant cities in order to harass and harm him. Here, once more, the message about their Messiah had been rejected. God knew that if Paul needed anything, it was encouragement. He knew also that he needed added courage.

Discouragement can lead to fear—a fact that every counselor needs to understand. Many counselees give evidence of this debilitating mix. So the Lord Jesus came to Paul in a vision to encourage and strengthen him. He said the following, **"Don't be afraid. Keep on speaking** (Had Paul been on the verge of giving up?). **I am with you. Nobody will attack you to harm you. And I have many people in this city**." These were wonderful words that surely must have greatly encouraged the apostle. You and your counselees can expect no visions to bring encouragement. But you have the marvelous promises of God recorded in the Scriptures, which in many ways ought to be even more encouraging. Next, we read that Paul settled in Corinth for a year and a half preaching the Word (vv. 9-11). A

9   In a night vision the Lord said to Paul,
          Don't be afraid. Keep on speaking; don't be silent.
10   I am with you, and nobody will attack you to harm you, because I
          have many people in this city.
11   Then he settled there a year and a half, teaching God's Word among
them.
   12   When Gallio was proconsul of Achaia, the Jews unitedly attacked
Paul and dragged him to the tribunal, saying,
13   "This man is inciting people to worship God contrary to the law."
14   As Paul was about to open his mouth, Gallio said to the Jews,
          If indeed it were some crime or vicious misdeed, I'd accept your
          complaint, you Jews,
15   but since it is a matter about words and names and your own law,
          see to it yourselves. I don't intend to become a judge of these
          things.
16   So he drove them away from the tribunal.

---

church was developed there and grew rapidly. Where there is favorable
response, it is usually time to settle down to do long term work. Paul also
needed a more settled situation after being chased over half of Asia
Minor! God knows what we need, and He is able and willing to provide it.
Count on that in counseling and teach your counselees to do so.

   The success in Corinth was interrupted at length by the united efforts
of Jews who didn't want to see any more church growth (v. 12). They
dragged Paul before the proconsul of Asia, **Gallio**, claiming that he had
been **inciting people to worship God contrary to the law**. But before
Paul was able to speak, Gallio told them that he wanted no part of their
Jewish controversies, and he drove them away (vv. 12-16). So they
grabbed Sosthenes, the synagog ruler, who must also have gone over to
the Christians after Crispus did, and beat him in front of the tribunal. Gallio ignored their actions. The fury of the Jews was so great that they
seemed to have vented it on the first Christian of note that they could lay
their hands on. Confused sinners, blinded by rage, are likely to do most
anything. Counselees should look for irrational behavior, wild lashing out
(physically or verbally), and the like by those who think that they have
reason to object to the gospel. Show counselees who have been viciously
attacked in such ways that, as in the case before us, this is the result of the
frustration of not obtaining what they want.

   Paul, for some reason,[1] did not suffer physical harm at their hands

---

[1] That is, for some reason on the part of the Jews. We know the ultimate reason (v. 10).

17 Then they all grabbed Sosthenes, the synagog ruler, and beat him in front of the tribunal, but Gallio didn't care at all about it.

18 After Paul stayed there many days, he said good-bye to the brothers and sailed off for Syria, together with Priscilla and Aquila. At Cenchrea he cut his hair because he took a vow.

19 They went down to Ephesus, where he left them. And he went into the synagog and reasoned with the Jews.

---

and was able to remain there for some time. Taking Aquila and Priscilla with him, Paul eventually sailed off for Syria. At Cenchrea, he cut his **hair** as a sign that he had taken a **vow** upon himself. As J.A. Alexander says, before the destruction of the temple in 70 AD, the observance of aspects of the ceremonial law was still legitimate. What the vow was or why Paul took it, we do not know. But in working among the Jews, he would be more likely to be able to win some if he followed the harmless custom. After all, he knew that it had nothing to do with his salvation or sanctification. He was exercising his Christian liberty in the matter.

Arriving in Ephesus, Paul received a warm welcome. People asked him to stay longer, but he couldn't (v. 20). But he promised to return. Which, of course, he did. Finally, he arrived in Caesarea, where he greeted the church; he went next to Antioch, which had been his destination (vv. 21, 22). He spent quite some time here at his home church. Then Paul went back to Galatia and Phrygia, **strengthening all the disciples** (v. 23; cf. 14:22). On this third mission Paul next went to **Ephesus** according to his promise, even though the facts about his travel was postponed until 19:1. An interesting incident occurred in Ephesus.

Luke provides an interlude in which he describes what had happened in Ephesus, presumably while Paul was in Antioch. An Alexandrian whose name was **Apollos** came to Ephesus. He was an eloquent speaker, but his doctrine was defective in some respects. In many ways he taught **powerfully** in the synagog. Aquila and Priscilla, who must have remained behind in Ephesus, took him aside and **explained God's Way . . . more accurately** (v. 26). Having learned from them what he needed to know, Apollos determined to go to Achaia and was able to take with him letters from the brothers in Ephesus. Evidently his defects were remedied. As a result, he was very helpful to Christians in Achaia (especially, it seems in Corinth; 19:1). He was a strong opponent of unbelieving Jews whom he refuted **in public, proving by the Scriptures that Jesus was the Christ**. But, as we shall see in the next chapter, he left behind other Ephesian dis-

20 But when they asked him to stay for a longer time, he couldn't agree to it;

21 instead, he said good-bye and promised, "I'll come back to you again if God wants me to." Then he sailed from Ephesus.

22 When he landed at Caesarea, he went up and greeted the church and then went down to Antioch.

23 After spending some time there, he left and went from place to place throughout the country of Galatia and Phrygia, strengthening all the disciples.

24 Now a certain Jew, named Apollos, who was a native of Alexandria, came to Ephesus. He was an eloquent man who powerfully expounded the Scriptures.

25 He had been orally instructed in the Lord's Way, and with great fervency he spoke and taught accurately the facts about Jesus, but he knew only John's baptism.

26 And he began to preach boldly in the synagog. So when Priscilla and Aquila heard him, they took him aside and explained God's Way to him more accurately.

27 And when he wanted to go to Achaia the brothers encouraged him and wrote to the disciples to welcome him. When he arrived he contributed a great deal to those who had believed through grace.

28 He vigorously refuted the Jews in public, proving by the Scriptures that Jesus was the Christ.

---

ciples also defective in their beliefs.

There is a place for helping those who are genuine Christians[1] but simply don't have it all together. The answer is not to immediately brand them as wrong, to be avoided, or the like. First try to help them as Aquila and Priscilla did. The letters that were sent by the church at Ephesus indicated that Apollos listened, learned and profited from that instruction. To postulate either a jealous or doctrinal antagonism between Paul and Apollos is decidedly wrong. It was Paul's own disciples who instructed him and who recommended him to the church in Corinth (v. 27). One of the principal tasks for a Christian counselor is to help people see truths in the Bible that they previously did not see. Correcting and instructing is, indeed, a counselor's task (cf. Isaiah 40:13, 14). Those who are helped by him may be used mightily in the propagation of the faith (vv. 27, 28).

---

[1] Apollos has been wrongly accused of heresy and even of founding Gnosticism!

CHAPTER 19

1 While Apollos was in Corinth Paul, traveling by the upper route, came to Ephesus. He found some disciples
2 and said to them, "Did you receive the Holy Spirit when you believed?" They replied, "No, we haven't even heard that there is a Holy Spirit."
3 So he said, "Into what, then, were you baptized?" They said, "Into John's baptism."
4 Paul said, "John baptized with a baptism of repentance, telling the people to believe in the One coming after him—in Jesus."
5 When they heard this, they were baptized into the name of the Lord Jesus.
6 As Paul laid his hands on them, the Holy Spirit came upon them, and they spoke in different languages and prophesied.

The first part of this chapter relates to the interlude in the last few verses of the previous chapter (vv. 24-28). Apollos' teaching had been defective until he was better informed by Aquila and Priscilla. His influence had been widespread it seems. Upon coming to Ephesus in fulfillment of his promise, Paul found some **disciples** (converts of Apollos we may assume[1]) who had come to faith in Christ, but only by route of John the Baptist's preaching. They had been baptized **into John's baptism** but had not received *Christian* baptism or what it represented, the baptism of the Holy Spirit. Because the baptism of John and the baptism of Jesus were not equivalent, Paul baptized them into the name of the Lord Jesus. Then, by the **laying on of** apostolic **hands**, they received the Holy Spirit (vv. 1-7), as did the crowd at Pentecost.[2]

This was not a rebaptism. The essential question asked by Paul, **"Into what, then, were you baptized?"** is the one we must always ask about anyone's baptism. It reaches to the heart of a baptism's validity. Sometimes people want to know whether Roman Catholic or cultic baptism is acceptable. The critical issue in determining the answer to this question is found in these words: **into *what*[3]** *was the person baptized?*

---

[1] Or, possibly, Apollos could simply have been associated with these twelve men.

[2] Many of whom had also received John's baptism (he had prepared them for the coming of Christ).

[3] That is "toward (*eis*) what end" (or *for* what purpose).

7   All together there were about twelve men.

8   And he went into the synagog and spoke boldly for three months, reasoning and persuading about God's empire.

9   But when some became hardened and disbelieved, saying bad things about the Way before the group, he withdrew from them, taking the disciples apart, and he reasoned daily at Tyrannus' school.

10   This continued for two years, so that all who were living in Asia—both Jews and Greeks—heard the Lord's Word.

What was the meaning and the purpose of the baptism? If John's legitimate (though negative) baptism was not an adequate substitute for Christian baptism (which was positive as well as negative), surely one which never was legitimate in the first place isn't adequate either. Roman Catholic baptism, for instance, is for *the purpose of* forgiving and cleansing from original sin. That isn't, and never was, a correct understanding or legitimate purpose for baptism. Indeed, that unscriptural purpose detracts from the cleansing power of the cross. The Roman Catholic was never baptized with Christian baptism; he therefore must be baptized for the first time upon conversion. Matters like these may be somewhat rare in counseling, but the counselor must be prepared to deal with them whenever they arise.

The Jews in Ephesus listened to Paul teach in their synagog as be **spoke boldly for three months**. That was a better reception than he experienced almost anywhere else. Again, he is represented as **reasoning and persuading**. He was giving his heart and soul to the task of winning these Jews[1] (v. 8). But then some became **hardened and disbelieved**; so together with his converts, Paul left them and taught **daily at Tyrannus' school**. He continued there for two years, and the message spread all over Asia Minor to both Jews and Greeks. Ephesus had become a center from which to promote the faith!

After repeatedly hearing the truth, there are those who in time either believe or become **hardened** (as Pharaoh did) to the message. The same is often true of disobedient counselees. When they begin to speak disparagingly about the faith, it is time to **withdraw from them** as well[2] (v. 9).

---

[1] Those who reject reasoning and persuading, it seems, rarely give themselves to others as Paul did.

[2] The answer for supposed Christians who act this way is church discipline (Matthew 18:15ff.).

11 God did extraordinary miracles by Paul's hands,

12 so that even handkerchiefs and aprons that had been in contact with his skin were taken to the sick, and they were cured of their diseases and evil spirits left them.

13 Then some of the traveling Jewish exorcists tried to pronounce the name of the Lord Jesus over those who had evil spirits, saying, "I exorcise you by the Jesus that Paul preaches."

14 There were seven sons of a Jewish high priest named Sceva who were doing this.

15 But the evil spirit answered them, "I know Jesus, and I know Paul, but who are you?"

16 Then the man who had the evil spirit jumped on them and so overpowered them all that they fled from the house naked and wounded.

17 And this became known to everybody who lived in Ephesus, both Jews and Greeks, and fear fell over all of them and the name of the Lord Jesus was held in respect.

There is no percentage in debating them. Of course, if they are true Christians in a disobedient and rebellious mode, they still possess the Spirit, and there is a possibility that they may repent. Here in the text we are talking about how Paul responded to hardened unbelievers.

Paul not only taught, but also performed miracles which are enumerated in verses 11 and 12. In time some traveling **Jewish exorcists** came to town. Seeing Paul's miracles that were done in Christ's Name, they too tried to use the Name of the Lord Jesus for exorcism, but in a magical way. It was seven of a high priest's sons who attempted this. But the evil spirit would have none of it. He knew Jesus and Paul, he said, but not them. They had no authority over him is what the spirit's words meant. So the demon caused the possessed man to jump on and overpower them. He was so powerful that they fled from the house wounded having had their clothes ripped off them. This incident became widely known so that everyone began to hold Jesus' Name in high respect (vv. 14-17). From time to time incidents—such as the successful counseling of a person no one thought could be helped—also will bring great respect to the Name of Jesus. That is the main reason that biblical counseling is important; we want others to recognize that Christ can do what the counsel of unbelievers cannot. In so doing, we want to see people drawn to Him. It is altogether important, then, for biblical counselors to be able to counsel with power from God's Word.

A great public display took place shortly after this event. Sponta-

18 Now many of those who had believed came, confessing and relating their practices.

19 And a number of those who had been practicing magic brought their books together and burned them publicly. They counted the value of these and it totaled fifty thousand pieces of silver.

20 So in this way the Lord's Word grew mightily and in strength.

21 Now after these things had taken place, Paul by the Spirit decided to pass through Macedonia and Achaia and go to Jerusalem, telling himself, "After I have been there, I must see Rome, too."

22 After sending Timothy and Erastus, two of his helpers, he himself stayed in Asia for a time.

23 Now about that time there arose no little disturbance over the Way.

24 A silversmith named Demetrius, who made silver statuettes of Artemis, brought no little trade to the craftsmen.

25 Gathering them together, with workmen of similar trades, he said,
   Men, you know that our wealth comes from this business.

26 But you see and hear how, not only in Ephesus but in almost all of Asia, this Paul has persuaded and perverted a good-sized crowd, saying that gods made by hands are not gods.

27 There is danger, not only that our business may fall into disrepute, but that the temple of the great goddess Artemis may be considered to be nothing, and that she, whom all of Asia and the whole world worships, may be dethroned from her majesty.

---

neously, converts to the faith came and **confessed** how they had previously trusted in **magic** and false gods. They brought their magic books and held a public **burning** of them[1] (vv. 18, 19). Doubtless this impressed many, and the Word of God **grew mightily because of** all these things.

In time, the **Spirit** directed Paul to leave Ephesus and to travel to **Jerusalem** by means of Macedonia and Achaia. He also had in mind at length to go to Rome. But he sent some of his helpers ahead and ministered for a time in Asia Minor. Before he left, Paul was embroiled in an incident with **Demetrius**, the **silversmith**, whose occupation was threatened by the fact that Paul's converts no longer bought the silver statuettes of Artemis (Diana) that he manufactured. He gathered other tradesmen of a similar sort together and incited them against Paul. He was right in saying that Paul had persuaded many to believe that **the gods made by hands were not gods** (v. 26). Demetrius' motives were clear: **"there is danger that our businesses may fall into disrepute."** Then, he added

---

[1] Presumably, a reckoning of the worth of these books was taken (v.19).

28 When they heard this they were filled with anger and shouted, "Great is Artemis of the Ephesians!"

29 So the city was filled with confusion, and they unitedly rushed into the theatre, dragging along the Macedonians Gaius and Aristarchus, who were Paul's traveling companions.

30 Paul wanted to go into the crowd, but the disciples wouldn't let him.

31 Some of the Asiarchs too, who were his friends, sent word urging him not to risk going into the theatre.

32 Now some shouted one thing, and some shouted another, because the assembly was in confusion and most of them didn't know why they had come together.

33 Some of the crowd prompted Alexander, whom the Jews had put forward, and Alexander motioned with his hand and tried to make a defense to the mob.

34 But when they learned that he was a Jew, they all shouted as one man for about two hours, "Great is Artemis of the Ephesians!"

35 When the town clerk had quieted the crowd, he said,

> Men of Ephesus, who is there who doesn't know that the city of Ephesus is the custodian of the temple of the great Artemis and of her image that fell from the sky?

---

some piously hypocritical words to the effect that poor Artemis may **be dethroned from her majesty** (v. 27).

The group were whipped up into a fury and began shouting, **"Great is Artemis of the Ephesians!"** They evidently went around the city doing this until the whole city was stirred. Crowds rushed into the **theater** grounds **dragging along the traveling companions who were still with Paul**. Paul wanted to go into the crowd, but the brothers wouldn't let him. Even some of the officials, who had become his friends, urged him not to go (vv. 28-31).

It is interesting that in the three years that he was at Ephesus,[1] Paul had made fast friends with officials of the city while planting a church. Those who are skillful in their work will stand before rulers and not before obscure people (Proverbs 22:29). Counselors, faithful in their tasks, will find that they have made an impact far beyond their dreams.

The **assembly** was a motley bunch. Many had no idea why they had come together. It was simply mob spirit that drove most of them into the theater. Alexander, a Jew, tried to speak. But when they learned he was a Jew, who as such also disbelieved in idolatry, they shouted him down and

---

[1] Two years in Tyrannus' school after an initial year of activity.

36   Since these things are undeniable, you ought to remain quiet and do nothing rash.

37   You dragged these men here, who are neither temple robbers nor blasphemers of your goddess.

38   So if Demetrius and those craftsmen who are with him have a complaint against anybody, the courts are in session and there are proconsuls; let them bring charges against them.

39   If you want to do something further, it will be settled in a lawful assembly.

40   I say this because we are in danger of being charged with rioting for what we have done today, since there are no grounds that we can give to account for this commotion.

41   When he had said this, he dismissed the assembly.

---

wouldn't let him speak. But then the **town clerk** quieted and appeased them by saying, "**who is there who doesn't know that the city of Ephesus is the custodian of the temple of the great Artemis and of her image that fell from the sky?**" Then he urged them to be quiet and go about their business. They had acted unlawfully, he pointed out, by dragging men to the theater who had committed no crime. Then he told them that if Demetrius and his fellow rabble rousers had a **complaint**, they should lodge it **lawfully**. And he warned them that they were all in danger of **being charged with rioting. . . since there** were **no grounds. . . for** the **commotion**. Often God uses the reasonable law enforcing agencies of the state to preserve His servants from harm. With Paul (Romans 13) we can thank God for them and honor them even when they themselves do not act honorably. Counselees who think otherwise may need instruction in these matters.

CHAPTER 20

1 After the uproar had subsided, Paul sent for the disciples, and having encouraged them, he said good-bye and departed for Macedonia.

2 When he had gone through those parts and spoken many encouraging words to them, he went to Greece.

3 He spent three months there, and since a plot was made against him by the Jews as he was about to sail for Syria, he determined to return through Macedonia.

4 Sopater from Berea, Pyrrhus' son, Aristarchus and Secundus from Thessalonica, Gaius from Derbe, Timothy and Tychicus and Trophimus from Asia, accompanied him.

5 They went on and waited for us in Troas,

6 while we sailed from Philippi after the Days of Unleavened Bread, and in five days we rejoined them at Troas, where we stayed for seven days.

7 On the first day of the week, when we were gathered together to break bread, Paul reasoned with them, and since he was going to leave the next day, he continued his talk till midnight.

8 Now there were quite a few lamps in the upper room where we had assembled.

The **uproar** mentioned in verse 1 was the one in which the city assembled in the theater. The town clerk calmed the people and sent them home. Paul then left Ephesus after farewell greetings to the brothers in the church there and headed for Macedonia (v. 1). He spent some time in Greece and, because a **plot** had been cooked up by the Jews who were still out to kill him, he changed his route and went back through Macedonia rather than going directly to Syria (vv. 2, 3). By now he had quite a large group of persons traveling with him (their names are mentioned in v. 4). Luke and others met them in **Troas** (vv. 5, 6). There, because the church gathered on the first day of the week, Paul preached until midnight the night before he left. During his sermon **Eutychus**, a young man, grew drowsy and fell down from the third floor and died. The fumes from the lamps exiting through the window (v. 8) may have led to this, but we don't know (surely it wasn't Paul's preaching!). At any rate, Paul threw himself on the boy and he revived. Then they ate together and talked until daybreak, and Paul and his company left.

Tragedies that occur among the brothers are opportunities to **encourage** the flock (v. 12). Of course we expect no resurrections of those who

9   And a certain young man named Eutychus, who was sitting on a window sill, became drowsy as Paul reasoned still longer, and because he was drowsy he fell down from the third floor. And when they picked him up, he was dead.

10   But Paul went down and threw himself on him and tightly embraced him and said, "Don't be alarmed; his life is in him."

11   Then he went up and broke bread and ate, and talked with them for a long time, till daybreak; then he left.

12   And they took the boy away alive and were enormously encouraged.

13   We went ahead to a ship and sailed for Assos, where we were going to take Paul aboard. We arranged this because he was going to go by foot.

14   So when he met us at Assos, we took him aboard and went to Mitylene.

15   The next day we sailed from there and arrived at a point off Chios. The following day we crossed over to Samos, and the day after we came to Miletus.

16   Paul had decided to sail past Ephesus to avoid spending time in Asia, since he was hurrying to be in Jerusalem, if possible, by the Day of Pentecost.

17   So from Miletus he sent word to Ephesus for the elders of the church.

18   When they came to him, he said to them,

>   You know what I was like the whole time that I was with you,
>   from the first day that I set foot in Asia,

---

have died (until Christ returns), but there can be good outcomes that equally strengthen and encourage the body. It is a counselor's task, when dealing with tragedies, to point this out and help his counselees look for and rejoice in the good that God will bring out of a tragedy.

Probably to avoid the plot mentioned above, Paul determined to go by foot to Assos where Luke and others, who were sailing, met him and took him on board (v. 13). They stopped at several ports along the way. But at Miletus,[1] where they harbored, Paul sent for the **elders** of the Ephesian church (v. 17); they came to him as the ship was preparing to sail. Here a very instructive and moving scene was enacted as they said good-bye for the last time.

As he looked back over the three year ministry in Ephesus,[2] Paul then spoke. (This is the only sermon in Acts delivered to a Christian gath-

---

[1] The seaport for Ephesus.

[2] Paul was more of a pastor here than elsewhere.

19	serving the Lord with true humility and tears during trials that happened to me as the result of Jewish plots;
20	that I didn't hold back in declaring anything that was beneficial to you and in teaching you publicly and from house to house.

ering.)[1] He reminded them of his ministry among them. He recalled the Jewish plots and the suffering that these occasioned (v. 19). He also referred to his humility and his tears for them in Christ's service. It was not a lack of humility for Paul to mention his humility; since it was true humility, they knew it and needed to be reminded of it so that they would emulate it. There are times and places and gatherings of people in which it would not be appropriate to mention these things. Counselors are supposed to be filled with wisdom and good judgment; they are supposed to be able, therefore, to distinguish between different occasions. And they must be able to help counselees make such decisions.

Then he described the ministry that he had among them. He said that he didn't **hold back in declaring anything that was beneficial** (v. 20). The word translated **hold back** (here and in v. 27) is, literally, "furl."[2] It means to fold up and stow away. Here in this nautical setting it was probably suggested by Paul's surroundings. That is an important note. Every biblical ministry is characterized by the same truth. A true servant of Christ never withholds anything—whether it be pleasant or unpleasant—from those to whom he preaches. He unfurls it all. It is the hireling who, in order to preserve his job, hedges and waffles. A counselor ought to make it his purpose to be sure that he offers *everything* **beneficial** that the Scriptures say about a situation to counselees who find themselves in it. A man who refuses to do so because of personal advantage isn't worthy of the ministry.

Note also, according to verse 20, Paul did not merely preach **publicly**, but he was engaged in private counseling as well in the homes of the Ephesians. Those who are interested in preaching only and avoid doing counseling need to study this chapter carefully. If they gain an Acts 20/20 vision of the ministry they will alter this perspective.

What Paul preached was a solemn message of **repentance** toward an

---

[1] Though a specialized one since they were all elders of the several congregations in Ephesus.

[2] The opposite of our "unfurl" a word that we still use, though *furl* has become obsolete.

21 I solemnly testified both to Jews and to Greeks about repentance toward God and faith toward our Lord Jesus.

22 Now, the fact is, I am going to Jerusalem, bound by the Spirit, not knowing what I am going to face there,

23 except that the Holy Spirit testifies to me, saying that in city after city bonds and afflictions await me.

24 But I don't count my life of any value to me, so long as I can finish my course and complete the ministry that I received from the Lord Jesus, to testify thoroughly to the good news of God's grace.

---

offended God and **faith** toward a loving Savior Whom God had provided for them (v. 21). Too often the message of faith crowds out the message of repentance. Repentance means that a person confesses that he has offended God by his unrighteous thoughts and ways and then turns in faith toward the Son of God Whom God sent to save him. It means a change of mind that leads to a change of life. Both are necessary since our ways as well as our thoughts are not God's ways and thoughts (Isaiah 55:8).

Looking ahead, Paul told them he was going to **Jerusalem** where the Spirit had sent him (19:21). Indeed, he said that it was as if the Spirit had bound him and was taking him as a prisoner to Jerusalem. He knew that difficult times were ahead because the Spirit told him that there were afflictions in city after city awaiting him. Exactly what would happen in Jerusalem he didn't know, but he was prepared to face it. If he died, he died. The key thing for him was that he would serve Christ fully (vv. 22-24). That attitude ought to brim over in the heart of all who seek to minister for Christ. Many have an altogether too "professional" attitude toward ministry. There must rather be a heartfelt commitment to Christ. Ministry is not merely a "job."

Paul told them that this was the last time they would see one another and that as he left them, he was clean of everybody's **blood**. He had faithfully ministered among them so that if they failed to believe, or if they failed to live as they should, that was their fault. His ministry had been complete, with nothing **beneficial** lacking. You must be able to say the same, counselor. Can you? Will you be able to at the conclusion of your ministry? That is an important consideration.

Again he said he furled nothing, but declared **God's whole counsel** to them. And he went on to exhort them as elders to carry on their work with fidelity. He told them to **Pay attention** to their own lives and to the lives of the whole flock. How they lived and how they helped the flock to

25 And now I know as a fact that all of you among whom I went preaching about the empire won't see my face again.

26   So then, I testify to you this day that I am clean from everybody's blood,

27   because I haven't held back in declaring God's whole counsel to you.

28 Pay attention to yourselves and to all of the flock among which the Holy Spirit has set you to be overseers to shepherd God's church,[1] that He acquired with His own blood.

29   I know that after my departure fierce wolves will enter in among you, not sparing the flock,

30   and from among yourselves men will arise speaking distorted things to drag away disciples to follow them.

31   Therefore, be alert, remembering that for three years, night and day, I didn't stop counseling each one of you with tears.

---

[1] Some MSS read, *the Lord's church.*

---

do so was of prime importance. There are members of the flock today who think that it is none of the business of the elders of the church to be concerned about how they live. Here God, through Paul, makes it every elder's responsibility to care not only about how well his own life accords with God's requirements but also how that of each member's does. Counselors have a mandate from God to "meddle" in the lives of their flock. They are to be shepherdly **overseers**.[1]

Then Paul warned them that from within and from without the flock, **wolves** would arise not sparing the flock. This problem arises at some time in almost every congregation today as well. Counselors should alert elders to the task of protecting the flock from their incursions. These wolves will devour congregations if they are given any leeway at all (cf. Titus 3:10). Spiritual wolves must be handled as Psalm 23 suggests—by means of the rod and staff!

Verse 31 sets forth a clear description of the counseling ministry. For three years (the whole time he was there), night and day (he was always available) Paul didn't stop counseling (lit., nouthetically confronting) each one (in an individualized ministry) with tears (out of deep concern for each one). I could write a book on each of those elements of the coun-

---

[1] For details on this see my book *Shepherding God's Flock.*

32   And now, I commend you to God and to His helpful Word that is able to build you up and give you an inheritance among all those who have been set apart.

33 I didn't desire anybody's silver or gold or clothing.

34   You yourselves know that these hands ministered to my needs and to the needs of those who were with me.

35   In every way I showed you that by such laboring one must help the needy, remembering the words of the Lord Jesus, Who said, "It is more blessed to give than to receive."

36 So when he had spoken these things, he knelt down and prayed with them all.

37 They wept a great deal, and they embraced Paul and fervently kissed him,

38 especially grieving over the word that he had spoken that they weren't going to see his face any more. Then they escorted him to the ship.

---

seling ministry.[1] But it is beyond my scope here. Let me say that every would be counselor ought to read every commentary he can find on this verse, totally familiarizing himself with every aspect of it. Have you read Calvin? Are you ready to expound this verse for everyone who wonders about your counseling ministry.

As he concluded, Paul commended them all to God *and His helpful Word*. Notice what the apostle left with the church. That is what we have today to depend upon—God and the Bible! And it is enough. The **help** that one needs in life is found in the Word. Paul did not encourage the Ephesians to depend on the Word and Stoicism or Epicureanism. He commended them into the hands of God Who gives help through His Word. Clearly, it is through that Word that they would be able to be **built up** in their faith; it would lead them unerringly to that **inheritance** that is for all believers (v. 32).

Finally, he urged them to follow his example of industry rather than live lives dependent on others. This is a needed note in our day of welfare and whining. Then they all prayed, wept and embraced one another. The elders grieved over the fact that they would see him no more. This is the sort of relationship that every pastor ought to have with his board of elders. There should be rich, mutual affection between them. They then escorted Paul to the ship.

---

[1] Come to think of it, some day I might.

CHAPTER 21

1   When we had torn ourselves away from them, we set sail and, taking a straight course, we came to Cos, the next day to Rhodes and from there to Patara.

2   Then, having found a ship crossing over to Phoenicia, we went aboard and set sail.

3   When we sighted Cyprus on our left, we passed it, sailed to Syria and landed at Tyre, because the ship was to unload its cargo there.

4   We looked for the disciples and stayed there seven days. They told Paul through the Spirit not to go up to Jerusalem.

5   But when our days there had come to an end, we left and went on our journey. All of them—even wives and children—escorted us until we were outside of the city. Then, kneeling down on the beach, we prayed and said good-bye to one another.

6   Then we went aboard the ship, and they returned home.

7   When we had completed the voyage from Tyre, we arrived at Ptolemais, greeted the brothers and stayed one day with them.

8   Then, on the next day, we left and went to Caesarea. We entered the house of Philip the evangelist (who was one of the seven) and stayed with him.

9   He had four virgin daughters who prophesied.

From Ephesus, Paul and his companions traveled to Phoenicia, landing at **Tyre**. They looked up the Christians there and remained with them for seven days. Finally, they arrived at **Caesarea** where they stayed with **Philip the evangelist** (vv. 1-8). The camaraderie and fellowship in the early church in these pristine days is wonderful to observe. The hospitality, concern and interest that they had for one another is something that, for the most part, we in our age have not experienced. It might be well in counseling to stress these things, looking forward to the time when we might come to know these warm traits again, and urging counselees to become part of that revival. While there is always more excitement at the inception of something, that is no reason not to expect at least some approximation of the Christian concern that we have seen here. What happened once can happen again.

Agabus arrived and, taking Paul's belt, **bound** himself with it simulating Paul's imminent binding by the Jews at Jerusalem. He also prophesied that Paul would be handed over to the Gentiles by them (v. 11). Upon hearing this, everyone urged him not to go to Jerusalem. Paul replied, "**I**

10   We had stayed there for some days when the prophet Agabus came down from Judea.

11   He came to us and took Paul's belt and bound his own feet and hands and said, "This is what the Holy Spirit says: 'This is how the Jews at Jerusalem will bind the man who owns this belt, and they will hand him over to the Gentiles.'"

12   When we heard this, both we and those who lived there urged him not to go up to Jerusalem.

13   Then Paul answered, "What are you doing, crying and breaking my heart? I am ready not only to be bound, but even to die at Jerusalem for the name of the Lord Jesus."

14   So when he wouldn't be persuaded, we kept quiet and said, "The Lord's will be done."

15   Now after these days we got ready and went up to Jerusalem.

16   Some of the disciples from Caesarea also went with us and took us to the house of Mnason, a Cypriot and one of the early disciples, with whom we would stay.

17   When we arrived in Jerusalem, the brothers received us joyfully.

18   The next day Paul went with us to see James, and all the elders were present.

19   After greeting them, he related, one event after another, what God had done among the Gentiles through his ministry.

20   When they heard it, they glorified God and said to him,

---

am ready not only to be bound, but even to die." When they failed to persuade him, they said, "The Lord's will be done." Paul could do nothing else. Being **bound** by the Jews meant nothing to one who was already **bound** by the *Spirit* (20:22). When a person knows (from the Bible) what God's will is, he must not be deterred—even by the warnings of others who care. Often a counselee is diverted from pursuing a biblical course by friends and relatives. You must encourage him to obey God and not man (even well-meaning men). So Paul went and was well received by the **brothers** in Jerusalem (vv. 15-17).

Early on, Paul took the opportunity to visit with **James**. At this conference, the **elders** of the congregations in Jerusalem were present as well. It was a grand reception. Paul related what God had been doing among the Gentiles **through his ministry**. They all were thrilled and **glorified God**. But they also presented a problem. Here in Jerusalem, they said, **thousands** who still zealously kept the law had come to faith in Christ. They had heard that Paul had taught the Jews of the dispersion that

You see, brother, how many thousands of Jews there are who have believed. And all of them are zealous for the law.

21 But they have been told about you that you teach all the Jews who live among the Gentiles to abandon Moses, telling them not to circumcise their children and not to observe the customs.

22 What, then, should be done? They are certainly going to hear that you have come.

23 So, then, do what we tell you. We have four men who have taken a vow.

24 Take these men and purify yourself along with them and pay to have their heads shaved. Then everybody will know that there is nothing to what they have been told, but rather that you live in observance of the law.

25 But concerning the Gentiles who have believed, we have sent a letter giving our judgment that they should abstain from idolatrous sacrifices, blood, strangled animals and sexual sin.

26 Then, the next day, Paul took the men, purified himself with them and went into the temple to give notice of the date of the completion of the days of purification, at which time an offering had to be made for each one of them.

27 Now when the seven days were about to be completed, the Jews from Asia, who had seen him in the temple, stirred up all the crowd and laid their hands on him, shouting,

---

once they become believers they no longer need to do so[1] (vv. 20, 21). They wanted to know what to do about this. They would soon learn that Paul was there.

At length, they suggested a solution. Along with four men who had taken a vow, they were to purify themselves and shave their heads so that they would know that what they had been told was incorrect. There was no problem with reference to the Gentiles. They had sent the letter in which they already **gave their judgment** that the only requirement for them was that they should abstain from all practices connected with idolatry[2] (vv. 24, 25).

Paul was asked to band together with four men who had taken a Nazarite vow that was coming to an end (the sign that the seven days of purification were over was the shaving of the head), and he was asked to

---

[1] There is no evidence of this.

[2] Cf. Revelation 2:14, 20-22.

28 "Men of Israel, help! This is the person who is teaching everybody everywhere against the people and the law and this place. And not only that—he has also brought Greeks into the temple and made this holy place common!"

29 Previously, they had seen Trophimus the Ephesian in the city with him and supposed that Paul had brought him into the temple.

30 The whole city was aroused, the people rushed together, grabbed Paul, dragged him outside the temple grounds and instantly shut the doors.

31 As they were trying to kill him, word reached the commander of the Roman cohort that all Jerusalem was in an uproar.

32 At once he took soldiers and centurions and ran down to them. When they saw the commander and the soldiers, they stopped beating Paul.

33 Then the commander came up and arrested him and ordered him to be bound with two chains. He inquired who he was and what he had done.

34 But some of the crowd shouted one thing, and others something different; so, since he wasn't able to learn the facts because of the uproar, he gave orders to take him to the barracks.

35 But when he got to the steps, he had to be carried by the soldiers, because of the violence of the crowd;

36 a group of the people followed him, shouting, "Take him away!"

37 As Paul was about to be taken into the barracks, he asked the commander, "Would it be possible for me to say something to you?" And he answered, "Do you know Greek?

---

participate in their ceremony and to have his head shaved. This, James and the elders thought, should disabuse those who were concerned. Paul went along with this suggestion (v. 26), but it led to further complications.

Now some of Paul's sworn enemies from Asia Minor, who had caused him so much trouble, happened to be present in Jerusalem. They **stirred up the crowd**, shouting things against Paul and his teaching (v. 28). And then they accused him of bringing Greeks into the temple, thus defiling it! Here was Paul bending over backwards to identify himself with the Jewish population in order not to cause offense, and he was accused of doing the opposite! Counselees will present similar situations to you. But often their attitude will be different: "Here I make a herculean effort not to offend, and I get accused of doing the very thing that I tried to avoid—what's the use? You can't win for losing!" Paul took no such attitude.

These Jews from Asia Minor were so agitated that, at length, the entire city was **aroused**. The Jews dragged Paul outside the temple grounds and were set to **kill** him when the **commander** of the Roman

38 Then you aren't that Egyptian who previously stirred up a revolt and led the four thousand assassins out into the desert, are you?"
39 Paul said, "I am a Jew, a Tarsian from Cilicia, a citizen of no insignificant city. I beg you, let me speak to the people."

---

cohort and his soldiers, hearing of the riot, intervened (vv. 29-32). They **arrested** and **bound** Paul **with two chains**. The commander tried to find out the facts, but because of the uproar couldn't. All sorts of opinions were being tossed around. So he ordered his soldiers to take Paul to the barracks. Things were so unruly they had to carry Paul up the stairs. At the top Paul asked the commander whether it would be possible to say something. The commander was surprised that Paul addressed him in **Greek** and commented on the fact. He had supposed that Paul was the **Egyptian** who had previously caused some commotion by leading 4,000 men into the desert. Paul gave a quick sketch of his background, making it clear that he was a Roman citizen. Then he asked whether he might speak to the crowd. The commander agreed. What he said is contained in the next chapter.

This incident was, of course, part of the plan of God. It afforded an unparalleled opportunity for Paul to address a crowd of his fellow Jews concerning the Lord Jesus Christ. Rather than backing off and preserving his own life when he had been rescued by the Romans, we see that Paul was anxious to take advantage of the opportunity to bear witness to his Lord. There is a spirit in this that we have encountered throughout the book of Acts that reaches its climax here perhaps most profoundly. It can be described as a willingness to be whatever God wants, in whatever circumstance that may arise, just so long as there is an opportunity to witness for Christ. Something of the same spirit is precisely what many counselees need to adopt. Many of them find themselves in difficult situations. That is why they have come for counsel. Help them in danger and difficulty to focus on Christ and the gospel, not on self. They, with Paul, need to be encouraged to give themselves to the Lord to do His will, regardless of the outcome. When they acquire that sort of attitude not only will they have a good witness for Christ, but they will also be free from whining, complaining, bitterness and the like. It is the self-focus (so much a part of our age) that is debilitating.

Paul **motioned** with his hand, quieted the people enough to be heard, and then **addressed them in the Hebrew dialect** (actually Aramaic, which had become the language of Palestine since the return from the

40   When he had given permission, Paul stood on the steps, motioned with his hand to the people and, when there was a great silence, he addressed them in the Hebrew dialect, saying,

---

exile). This, as we shall see, gave him an even greater hearing as the crowd **became all the more quiet** (22:2). Even under these trying circumstances Paul adapts to the situation by switching between Greek (when speaking to the Roman) and Aramaic (when speaking to the Jews). He did not lose his head. He was ever the master strategist. Commitment doesn't only involve willingness; it also involves wittiness. Teach counselees that too. What they do in trouble is important; how they do it is equally as important. Many may do fairly well with the *what to*, but will bomb when it comes to the *how to*. Your task is to help them with both. Don't merely instruct them about *what* to do—and then leave them to mess up by *how* they do it. Discuss the right way to pull it off as well. Indeed, you might even find it helpful to role play the what to/how to with them to be sure that they have it right.

CHAPTER 22

1 "Brothers and fathers, listen to the defense that I now make to you."
2 When they heard that he was addressing them in the Hebrew dialect, they became all the more quiet. Then he said,

3   I am a Jew, born at Tarsus in Cilicia, but I was brought up in this city, educated at Gamaliel's feet, strictly according to the law of our fathers, with a zeal for God just like that which you all have today.

4   I persecuted this Way to the death, binding both men and women and delivering them to prison,

5   as the high priest and the whole presbytery can bear me witness. I received letters from them to the brothers in Damascus, to which I traveled to bring even those who were there bound to Jerusalem for punishment.

6   Now as I was traveling and drawing near to Damascus about noon, suddenly a great light from the sky flashed around me,

7   and I fell to the ground and heard a voice saying to me, "Saul, Saul, why are you persecuting Me?"

8   I answered, "Who are You, Lord?" He said to me, "I am Jesus the Nazarene, Whom you are persecuting."

9   Now those who were with me saw the light as well, but they didn't understand what the voice that spoke to me said,

---

Chapter twenty-two is a continuation of the incident that Luke began to relate in the previous chapter. Paul was rescued by the Roman commander from the angry mob that tried to kill him in the temple. He asked permission to speak to them. They responded to his initial words spoken in Aramaic. He addressed them as **brothers and fathers**, thereby identifying as closely as possible with them (vv. 1-2). Then, in verses 3 through 21, Luke records how Paul told his story (with a few additions, but essentially that which we read in chapter nine). Up until he said the word **Gentiles** they listened, but that word was the spark that set off the explosion. They **lifted up their voices and said, "A person like this should be removed from the earth! He isn't fit to live!"** Then they tore their garments and threw dust into the air (vv. 22, 23). This, of course, brought an end to the speech. You will find that certain words, phrases or ideas often trigger violent responses from counselees. Try to avoid using these unnecessarily. You may not always be able to, however, as Paul could not. When you must use them, try to get your main point across before the

10   I said, "What should I do, Lord?" Then the Lord said to me, "Get up and go to Damascus, and there you will be told about everything that has been arranged for you to do."

11   Since I couldn't see because of the glory of that light, I was led by the hand of those who were with me and went into Damascus.

12   A certain man named Ananias, devout by the standards of the law, well spoken of by all the Jews who lived there,

13   came to me and stood by me and said, "Brother Saul, look up and see," and at that very hour I looked up and saw.

14   He said, "The God of our fathers previously appointed you to know His will, to see the Righteous One and to hear a voice from His mouth.

15   This is because you will be His witness before all men of the things that you have seen and heard.

16   Now, what are you waiting for? Get up, be baptized, and wash away your sins, calling on His name."

17   When I had returned to Jerusalem, and was praying in the temple, I went into a trance,

18   and I saw Him saying to me, "Hurry, get out of Jerusalem quickly, because they won't accept your testimony about Me."

19   I said, "Lord, they know that I was going into all the synagogs, imprisoning and beating those who trust in You,

---

reaction occurs. Paul, like Stephen (whose death he mentions), was able to present the gospel before he was cut off. He held back the point of contention until he had virtually said all he needed to say. That is important in dealing with others. Also teach counselees to do this.

In verses 14 and 15 the qualifications for an apostle are set forth—an apostle must have seen the risen Christ and have a commission to tell others what he has witnessed. Because these qualifications cannot be met by anyone today, there are no apostles on earth. This is a point that is generally acknowledged, but the implications of it often are not. Regardless of claims to the contrary, the miracles that apostles did and the direct revelation that they received have ceased ever since the twelve died.[1] Those who seek such miracles or revelation should be made aware that these ceased because the apostles who imparted miraculous gifts by the laying on of their hands, and who received revelation because they were the sources for the future Bible, completed their work. That means that God's revelation to His church is complete (cf. I Corinthians 13:8-13).

---

[1] See discussions on Ephesians 2:20, etc.

20   and when the blood of Your witness Stephen was shed, I was standing there too, approving of it, and watching the clothes of those who were killing him."

21   But He said to me, "Go! I am going to send you far away to the Gentiles."

22 Up to that word they listened to him. Then they lifted up their voices and said, "A person like this should be removed from the earth! He isn't fit to live!"

23 They shouted and ripped off their clothes and threw dust into the air,

24 so the commander ordered him to be brought into the barracks, telling them to examine him with a whipping to find out exactly why they were shouting at him.

25 But as they were stretching him out to be tied with thongs, Paul said to the centurion, "Is it lawful for you to whip a Roman citizen uncondemned?"

26 When the centurion heard this, he went to the commander and said to him, "What are you about to do? This man is a Roman citizen."

27 So the commander went to him and said, "Tell me, are you a Roman citizen?" He said, "Yes."

28 Then the commander said, "I bought this citizenship at great cost." Paul said, "But I was born a citizen."

29 At once those who were about to examine him withdrew, and the commander also was afraid, because he realized that he was a Roman citizen and that he had bound him.

The commander brought Paul into the barracks before any more harm could be done to him. He ordered the soldiers to extract information from him by means of a whipping, but Paul protested, calling on his rights as a Roman **citizen** not to be subjected to such treatment. The centurion in charge of the examination informed the commander; he understood the privileges of citizenship very well, having paid a large sum to acquire his own citizenship. He immediately ordered them to cease and desist. He had even gone too far, he recognized, in having Paul **bound**. Indeed, he seems to have become downright chummy with Paul at this point. So, instead of interrogating Paul, he decided to find out in a different way what this commotion was all about. He released Paul, **ordered the chief priests and the entire Sanhedrin to meet** with him, and **brought Paul to stand before them** (vv. 24-30). The story continues in the next chapter.

Once more, we see Paul rightly asserting his rights. That counselees may do so too is something that we must understand if we would advise them correctly. There are those in the Christian world who say either that

30 So the next day, wanting to know for certain why the Jews accused him, he released him and ordered the chief priests and the entire Sanhedrin to meet. And he brought Paul to stand before them.

Christians have no rights, or that they always should "surrender" or "give up" their rights. While there certainly are occasions when one should relinquish certain rights, that is not universally true. Nor is it true that Christians have no rights. We are citizens of the state with its rights, and we are citizens of the Kingdom from the heavens with all the rights that appertain thereto. It is a matter of wisdom and prudence as to when one should assert his rights and privileges, as Paul did here, and when he should not. For more on this see I Corinthians 6 and 9 where Paul talks at length about such matters. It is important to reject seemingly pious exhortations that are not founded on Scripture (cf. Colossians 2:23); you must have a thoroughly biblical view of this matter. The counselor will be particularly useful to his counselees when he is able to help them distinguish between situations in which they should assert their rights and those in which they should not. When there is a judgment call in this matter, it is often necessary to invoke the holding principle (found in Romans 14[1]).When difficulty remains, the judgment of a board of elders may be called for. One of the functions of elders is to help members make judgment calls about how to apply the Scriptures on the basis of their wisdom, maturity and knowledge. Never hesitate to urge counselees to consult their elders.

---

[1] See the chapter on this in my book *The Christian's Guide to Guidance.*

CHAPTER 23

1 Paul looked straight at the Sanhedrin and said, "Brothers, I have lived before God with all good conscience to this day."
2 And Ananias, the high priest, ordered those who stood by him to strike him in the mouth.
3 Then Paul said to him, "God is going to strike you, you whitewashed wall! Are you sitting to judge me according to the law and commanding me to be struck contrary to the law?"
4 Those who stood by said, "Would you insult God's high priest?"
5 And Paul said, "Brothers, I didn't know that he was a high priest; after all, it is written, **You must not speak evil of a ruler of your people**."

We come now to Paul's confrontation with the **Sanhedrin**. For the fifth time the Sanhedrin, the highest religio-political court of the Jewish theocracy, had to adjudicate upon the claims of Christianity.[1] Never before had he known it to act justly. The bias of the court had been made only too clear by its previous words and actions. Its constituency was a corrupt, gluttonous, tyrannical crowd, perfectly exemplified by Ananias himself. They were deadly enemies of Christ and His church, both of which had bested them so far. They considered Paul an arch traitor. Paul, who had worked closely with them as their hatchet man, of course knew all of this.

Luke says that **Paul looked straight at the Sanhedrin.** In effect, he was putting **them** on trial! It is in this knowledge and in utter disdain that he stood before them and said, "**I have lived before God with all good conscience to this day**" (the emphasis being on the word **I** in the original). Ananias understood the contrast that Paul's emphasis on **I** was intended to convey, so he ordered Paul **to be struck in the mouth.** Having no desire to speak before this kangaroo court, Paul lashed back at him: "**God is going to strike you, you whitewashed wall!**" The principal judge's hypocritical act was too blatant to let go by, so Paul sharply pointed out that he had acted **contrary to the law.** Those who stood by asked Paul how he dared to speak about the High Priest in such language. Paul's reply is to the point: "**I didn't know that he was a high priest.**" Paul was in effect saying that everything about the man belied his posi-

---

[1] Jesus, Peter and John, Stephen, and James had all tried.

6 Then Paul, knowing that one part was Sadducees and the other was Pharisees, shouted out in the Sanhedrin, "Brothers, I am a Pharisee, a son of Pharisees! It is about the hope and the resurrection of the dead that I am being tried."

7　But when he said this, a dispute arose between the Pharisees and the Sadducees, and the group was divided.

8　This happened because the Sadducees say that there is no resurrection, nor angel nor spirit; but the Pharisees confess them all.

9　So there was a lot of noise. Some of the scribes of the part that was Pharisee stood up and fought for him, saying, "We don't find anything wrong with this man. What if a spirit or an angel spoke to him?"

---

tion, that he had no right to be in it and that he was not, in fact, a high priest of the true God.[1] His life and his actions had sufficiently proven this fact.

There are those who think that Paul was speaking out of ignorance or poor eyesight. No. His words are ironic. The deep, biting sarcasm of his reply was altogether appropriate. There was no way in which Paul could have literally failed to recognize the High Priest because of his dress and his position. Paul simply wouldn't acknowledge him as High Priest. Some think that it is never right to speak sharply to another. They are obviously wrong. Jesus did (cf. Matthew 23), and Paul did it here. When it is appropriate to do so, nothing less will suffice. Paul's words were fulfilled; Ananias met a miserable death. God struck him for his sin. He was dragged from a sewer, where in ignominy he was hiding for his life, and an assassin killed him.

Paul would not be tried by this court. So, knowing that the body was divided between Pharisees and Sadducees, he shouted, "**I am a Pharisee, a son of Pharisees! It is about the hope and the resurrection from the dead that I am being tried**."[2] Most of the Sanhedrin were Sadducees who did not believe in the resurrection, angels, or spirits. He hit on *the* issue between the two sects, purposely tossing the golden apple among them. The meeting broke up in noisy confusion that eventually became so violent that the commander had to remove Paul lest he be torn apart by the contending parties. What a religious group! No wonder Paul had no desire to be tried before them. As a matter of fact, in God's economy, they had

---

[1] Besides, the last High Priest had offered the final sacrifice on the cross!

[2] This was not a lie as some have thought. Always, everywhere, Paul had preached the resurrection. It was an essential element of the gospel.

10 The discord became so violent that the commander, fearing Paul would be torn apart by them, commanded the soldiers to go down and remove him from their midst and take him to the barracks.

11 The following night the Lord stood by him and said, "Take courage! As you have testified about Me in Jerusalem, so you must testify also at Rome."

12 When day came, the Jews plotted against him and bound themselves by oath in which they vowed neither to eat nor drink until they had killed Paul.

13 There were more than forty persons who were in on this plot.

14 They went to the chief priests and elders and said,

> We have bound ourselves with an oath to taste nothing till we have killed Paul.

15 Now, you and the Sanhedrin send word to the commander to have him bring Paul down to you, as though you were intending to determine his case more exactly, and we will be ready to kill him before he comes near.

16 But the son of Paul's sister heard about the ambush, so he went into the barracks and reported it to Paul.

17 Paul called one of the centurions and said, "Take this young man to the commander; he has something to report to him."

18 So he took him, and brought him to the commander and said, "Paul, the prisoner, called me and asked me to bring this young man to you, because he has something to tell you."

---

no right to exist because of their lack of integrity and because the Messiah had come. Since Calvary, their authority had been taken away and had been given to the church.

Paul had little hope of persuading this group (look at how they acted: vv. 3, 10). So by dividing them with this tactic, Paul avoided a formal, hostile decision against himself. From the outset (the **straightforward** look, the emphasis on *I*, the words that Paul shot back at Ananias, and the issue he raised), it is clear that Paul was baiting them to reveal their true colors. This was not a legitimate tribunal by any stretch of the imagination (vv. 1-10). Should a counselee ever come before such an illegitimate body, he would be permitted to act in a similar fashion. But he must be sure that he has as good reasons as Paul had for concluding it is without authority over him. In most cases, this will not be the situation.

Paul was at a critical point in his ministry. He had come to Jerusalem, and He had **testified** faithfully. Then the Lord appeared to him the night after his confrontation with the Sanhedrin and told him that he **must tes-**

19 The commander took him by the hand and, going privately, asked, "What is it that you have to report to me?"

20 He said,

> The Jews have agreed to ask you to bring Paul down to the Sanhedrin tomorrow, as though they were going to inquire more exactly about him.

21 > But don't let them persuade you to do this, since more than forty of their men are lying in ambush for him, who have bound themselves with an oath that they will neither eat nor drink until they kill him. Now they are ready, waiting for your promise.

22 Then the commander dismissed the young man, ordering him, "Don't tell anybody what you have reported to me."

23 Then he called two of the centurions and said,

> Get two hundred soldiers, seventy horsemen and two hundred spearmen ready to go to Caesarea at nine o'clock tonight.

24 > Provide mounts for Paul to ride and take him safely to Felix the governor.

25 And he wrote a letter containing the following words:

26 Claudius Lysias to his excellency the governor Felix, greeting.

27 > This man was seized by the Jews and was about to be killed by them when I came on the scene with my soldiers and rescued him, having learned that he is a Roman citizen.

28 > Wanting to know the exact grounds on which they were accusing him, I brought him down to their Sanhedrin.

---

tify also at Rome. Those who think that Paul acted wrongly before the Sanhedrin need to recognize that God accepted his **testimony** before them.[1] Let them do so too (v. 11).

The forty plus Jews who took an oath that they would neither eat nor drink until they had killed Paul (vv. 12-15) must have died a rather hungry and thirsty crowd! They never were able to lay their hands on him. Providentially Paul escaped from their clutches because of a leak that disclosed their plan (v. 16). Paul called one of the centurions and told him to take his nephew (who had informed him about the plot) to the commander; this he did. The commander got all of the facts, told the young lad to keep quiet about what he had done, and then spirited Paul away to the governor **Felix** in **Caesarea** under a guard of 200 soldiers, 70 horsemen and 200 spearmen. In his **letter** to Felix the commander omitted his hasty action of

---

[1] There is no hint of criticism in verse 11. Besides, this speech was Spirit inspired (cf. the discussion of this in chapter 2)!

29   I found that he was being accused about questions pertaining to their law, but charged with nothing worthy of death or imprisonment.

30   When it was disclosed to me that a plot had been formed against the man, I immediately sent him to you, also ordering his accusers to say what they have against him before you.

31 So the soldiers, according to their orders, took Paul and brought him by night to Antipatris.

32 Then the next day, they returned to their barracks, allowing the horsemen to go on with him.

---

binding Paul, mentioned the other facts of the case, and gave his judgment that Paul had done **nothing worthy of death** or even **imprisonment**. He correctly judged that this was a matter of Jewish **law** (vv. 28-30).

When it is His purpose to do so, God can providentially cause weak persons, government officials, or large bodies of men to preserve and protect His own. The king's heart is in His hand (see Proverbs 21:1). He may order him to act as He wills. Here, we see God at work through weak (a little lad) and powerful persons. He uses both. A counselee needs to know this. At bottom, it is not corrupt governmental or religious officials, it is not his boss, and it is not any other person who is causing him problems. Ultimately God, Who is in control of all things and all persons, is ordering the events. The counselee's hope and encouragement must rest on that fact. We have said it before: if the book of Acts teaches anything, it is that God is sovereign over the affairs of men, working out His will through them.

The soldiers took Paul as they had been ordered. At **Antipatris** the others turned back (since the plotters were far behind) and only the horsemen continued on the remaining 27-mile trip to Caesarea. Upon arrival, the governor read the letter, asked what province Paul was from, and told him that he would hear what he had to say when his accusers arrived. Paul was then put under guard. The efficiency of the orderly government of Rome is seen throughout this book, but especially in the handling of Paul in these present chapters. It contrasts vividly with the Jewish leadership.[1] We may thank God that we live under a government that (with all its problems) is also orderly. God has blessed us with this, and we should be as thankful for it as Paul was for his Roman citizenship. Too often we see

---

[1] There is a time, as we see here, when government becomes so disorderly that it is not worthy of the name or of submission to it.

33   When they went into Caesarea, they delivered the letter to the governor and presented Paul to him.

34   When he had read the letter, he asked, "From what province are you?" And when he learned that he was from Cilicia,

35   he said, "I will hear you when your accusers arrive." And he issued orders for him to be guarded in Herod's Praetorium.

---

only the bad side of the government. There were plenty of things wrong with the Roman rule that Paul could have complained about. Instead, as the Spirit led him to write, he mentioned only the good things (cf. his words about the government in Romans 13). Some counselees will have to undergo a basic adjustment of attitude toward the state before they can settle their problems with it.

CHAPTER 24

1   After five days Ananias, the high priest, came down with some elders and an orator named Tertullus, and they informed the governor about their charges against Paul.

2   When he had been called in, Tertullus began to accuse him, saying:
      Since we enjoy much peace through you, most excellent Felix, and since many reforms have come to this nation by your planning,

3   in every way and everywhere we welcome this with sincere gratitude.

4   But, not to detain you further, I urge you to kindly hear us briefly.

   5   We have found this man to be a pest who stirs up riots among all the Jews throughout the world. He is a ringleader of the sect of the Nazarenes,

6   who even tried to profane the temple, but we seized him.

7   1

8   By examining him about all of these things you will be able to learn fully about that which we have accused him.

---

[1] The latter part of vs. 6, all of vs. 7 and the first part of vs. 8 are omitted in the better MSS.

This chapter records the substance of two speeches: an obsequious one by **Tertullus**, a hired orator representing the Sanhedrin, and the explanatory defense by Paul. They stand in stark contrast. Tertullus called Paul a **pest** who had **stirred up riots among the Jews** all over the world. He claimed once more that Paul even tried to profane the temple. He urged Felix to **examine** him (by beating him) to learn the truth. The Jews joined with Tertullus in leveling accusations against Paul (vv. 1-9).

Then Paul spoke. His opening words were polite, but not obsequious as were Tertullus'. He appealed to easily ascertainable facts (vv. 11, 12). Witnesses could testify to them. He also challenged his opponents to **prove** the things they accused him of. He knew they could not. He did **admit** (as a way of presenting the gospel) that he had preached the truth of the **Way**[1] to which he adhered, and which was in accord with all the prophecies of the Old Testament. Moreover, he admitted holding to the

---

[1] This was the earliest name for the church.

150

9   The Jews joined in too, claiming that these things were true.

10 Then, when the governor had motioned for him to speak, Paul replied:

>   Realizing that for many years you have been a judge over this nation, I cheerfully make my defense.
>
> 11   You can ascertain the fact that it wasn't more than twelve days ago that I went up to worship at Jerusalem.
>
> 12   They didn't find me reasoning with anybody or gathering a crowd together either in the temple, in the synagogs or in the city.
>
> 13   Nor can they prove to you those things of which they now accuse me.
>
> **14** Now this is what I admit to you—that according to the Way (which they call a sect), I worship our fathers' God, believing what is according to the law and that which has been written in the prophets.
>
> 15   I hold to a hope in God that these men themselves accept, that there will be a resurrection of both the just and the unjust.
>
> 16   Because of this, also, I always make it a practice to have a blameless conscience before God and men.
>
> **17** Now, after a number of years, I came to bring alms and offerings to my nation.
>
> 18   In the midst of doing so, they found me purified in the temple, neither associated with a crowd nor with an uproar.

---

doctrine of the **resurrection**—which some of those before him, he observed, also accepted. But then he said that it was the **Jews from Asia Minor** (and asked where they were) who actually started the riot. And, he asked what was criminal about shouting that he believed in the **resurrection** from the dead before the Sanhedrin? He asked if that really was the reason they accused him before them? That was his simple, to the point, clear-cut, but powerful, defense (vv. 10-21).

Felix understood what Paul was talking about, since he knew about the **Way**. He said he would talk to **Lysias** the commander when he came and then would decide the case (v. 22), which he didn't do. He fully understood that Paul was not guilty. So he put Paul under house arrest, which allowed Paul a great deal of freedom in speaking with friends (v. 23). This gave Paul a ministry in that town to many for two years while he remained under arrest.[1]

---

[1] Cf. Paul's similar use of imprisonment in Philippians 1:12-14.

19   But some Jews from Asia—they are the ones who ought to be here before you to make an accusation if they have something against me.

20   Or else let these men tell you what crime they found when I stood before the Sanhedrin

21   (unless it is that one statement that I shouted while standing before them: "It is about the resurrection from the dead that I am being judged before you today").

22 But Felix, having a rather accurate knowledge of the Way, adjourned the hearing, saying, "When Lysias, the commander, comes down I will decide your case."

23 Then he ordered the centurion to guard him, but to give him some freedom and not to forbid any of his friends to attend to his needs.

24 Some days afterward, Felix came with his wife Drusilla, who was Jewish. He sent for Paul and listened to him about faith in Christ Jesus.

25 But as he reasoned with him about righteousness, self-control and the coming judgment, Felix became alarmed and replied, "Go away for now; when I have time later on, I'll send for you."

26 At the same time he hoped Paul would give him money; so he sent for him frequently and talked with him.

Felix listened to Paul **reason** about the essentials of the faith as he put them pointedly to him and his wife. But because he couldn't refute them, Felix became **alarmed** and put off seeing Paul until later, which he did more than once. (vv. 24-26). Here was a man toying with Christianity as many still do. But Luke never says that he believed. For two years this went on. But eventually when Felix was replaced by **Festus**, Paul was left in prison out of the latter's desire to win the good will of the Jews.

For all the wrong reasons God's people will be treated badly by others. The breakdown of the Roman order by corrupt and self-serving officials is highlighted here. The army seemed to have been in better shape than the rulers, as is so often the situation.[1] But Paul patiently kept up his faith and kept on talking to Felix, attempting to convert him. He did not become depressed during this time. He patiently waited for the Lord's will to play out. Under the circumstances, Paul's patience was exemplary.

Time in the life of Paul is interesting to study. We sometimes think of him as dashing here and there, blitzing the *oikoumene* with the gospel. Under the traveling conditions of the time, the territory he encompassed is truly remarkable. But we must also note the times when he waited some-

---

[1] Throughout the New Testament, centurions, for instance, get a good press.

27 But after two years had elapsed, Felix was succeeded by Porcius Festus, and because he wanted to do the Jews a favor, he left Paul in prison.

---

where for favorable sailing conditions to arise, the years he spent in prison, and the time he devoted to tentmaking. In God's providence He shelves His saints for His purposes. All is not feverish service. There is time for regrouping, earning money, thinking, resting—all of which are necessary, but all of which require and (if we are open to it) teach patience. Paul is a person to learn from in this respect.

CHAPTER 25

1 Three days after Festus had entered the province, he went up from Caesarea to Jerusalem.

2   And the chief priests and Jewish leaders made charges against Paul,

3   asking as a favor with reference to him to have him sent to Jerusalem, plotting to kill him along the way.

4   Festus replied that Paul was being kept in Caesarea, where he himself intended to go shortly.

5   "So," he said, "let some of your able men go down with me, and if there is anything amiss about the man, let them accuse him."

6 When he had stayed among them not more than eight or ten days, he went down to Caesarea, and the next day he took his seat in the court and issued orders for Paul to be brought.

7   When he arrived, the Jews who had come down from Jerusalem stood about him, making all sorts of serious charges against him that they couldn't prove.

8   Paul defended himself by saying, "I haven't committed wrong either against the Jewish law, against the temple or against Caesar."

Almost immediately upon the arrival of the new Roman governor Festus, the Jewish leaders revived the **charges** against Paul. They wanted him sent to Jerusalem, something Felix would not do. Now that there was a new governor, they thought they might at last attain their objective—to kill Paul along the road as he was being brought back to the city (vv. 1-3). Festus told them that Paul was in Caesarea where they should send their men to bring these charges against him. They responded by going to Caesarea and making all sorts of charges against him; but they couldn't prove them. Paul met each of the charges head on (vv. 4-8).

When people have a nefarious plan to execute, and hate someone enough, they will persist for even years in their attempts to execute it. The bitterness and resentment pent up in these men is almost unimaginable. Perhaps the mix of personal envy and hatred with religious bigotry is the most deadly combination of all. Be aware of it. Beware of it! They did not let up; they would not settle for Paul in jail indefinitely. They wanted him dead. Always be wary of someone who for years has persisted in attempting to do evil. You will probably get nowhere with him until there is genuine repentance and a thorough change of direction. Attempt to do nothing else until you have some evidence that repentance has occurred. And beware of him apart from repentance.

9 But Festus, wanting to do the Jews a favor, said to Paul, "Do you want to go up to Jerusalem and there stand trial about these charges before me?"

10 Paul said,

> I am standing trial in Caesar's court, where I ought to be tried. I haven't done anything wrong to the Jews, as you (of course) know quite well.

11 > If, then, I were a wrongdoer, and had done something worthy of death, I wouldn't try to escape death; but if there is nothing to their charges against me, nobody can hand me over to them as a favor. I appeal to Caesar!

Festus, having newly arrived, wanted to get on the good side of the Jews, who were very difficult to rule over since they were always stirring up some trouble or other. If he could **please** them at the outset, he thought, perhaps he would have a quiet governorship. So he asked Paul whether he might want to stand trial in Jerusalem. Paul understood what the Jews were after, so (once more asserting his rights as a Roman citizen[1]) he said, **"I am standing in Caesar's court where I ought to be tried. I haven't done anything wrong to the Jews, as you (of course) know quite well. If, then, I were a wrongdoer, and had done something worthy of death, I wouldn't try to escape death, but if there is nothing to their charges against me, nobody can hand me over to them as a favor—I appeal to Caesar."**

What a bold and thoroughly cogent speech. First, Paul let Festus know that he understood what he was up to. He wouldn't be used as his pawn to gain favor from the Jews. There are Christians who would never speak as Paul did. They would meekly (rather, weakly) go along with whatever happened, as though it were the Christian way to act. Not so. Paul would not be sacrificed to the whims of a corrupt Roman governor.

Second, it is interesting that Paul believed in the **death** penalty for any wrongdoing that was worthy of death. He said that he not only did not object to it, but he also would be willing to be put to death for a capital crime. Christians should have no qualms about serving on a jury that has to decide on a death penalty. Yet, in this day of frail Christianity impacted by worldly thinking, many Christians are undecided about the issue. Paul was not; neither you nor your counselees should be undecided either.

Last, once more we see that Paul knew his rights and had no hesita-

---

[1] Every citizen had the right to be judged by Caesar himself on appeal.

12 Then Festus, after consulting with his advisers, answered, "You have appealed to Caesar; to Caesar you will go."

13 After some days had gone by, Agrippa the king and Bernice arrived in Caesarea to welcome Festus.

14 Since they were staying there for quite a few days, Festus explained the situation regarding Paul to the king, saying,

There is a man who was left as a prisoner by Felix,

15   about whom the chief priests and the Jewish elders informed me when I was in Jerusalem, asking me to condemn him.

16   I told them that it isn't a Roman custom to hand over any person before the accused has met his accusers face to face and had an opportunity to defend himself against the charge.

17   So when they came together here, I didn't delay matters, but the next day took my seat in court and issued orders to bring the man.

18   When the accusers stood up, they didn't bring a charge of the sort of evils I had expected,

19   but they had differences with him about their own religion and about a certain Jesus who died, but whom Paul insisted was alive.

20   Since I was at a loss about how to investigate these matters, I asked whether he wanted to go to Jerusalem and there be tried about them.

21   But when Paul appealed to be kept in custody so that he could have a decision by the emperor, I gave orders to keep him until I can send him to Caesar.

---

tion about asserting them. I will not do more than mention this fact, since I have already discussed it at length. Suffice it to say that many Christians don't care enough about politics to know what their rights are. Paul appealed to Caesar. The appeal to Caesar was absolute. Upon making the appeal, all other proceedings came to a halt, and the appeal alone went forward. Festus, who probably was not as certain of the procedure as Paul seemed to be, had to consult with his advisers, who concurred with Paul. So Festus (probably glad to get Paul out of his hair, though disappointed in failing to satisfy his earlier intention of pleasing the Jews) said, "**You have appealed to Caesar; to Caesar you will go**" (v. 12). There must have been an exhilaration that shot through Paul's soul when he heard that declaration. Previously Paul had expressed his desire to preach in Rome. Later, Jesus had assured him that he would. Now it was about to happen.

Before Paul left, King **Agrippa** arrived to welcome Festus. Festus explained Paul's situation to him. He detailed the course of events that led to Paul's appeal (vv. 14-21) omitting, of course, his intention of throwing

22 Agrippa said to Festus, "I would like to hear the man myself." "Tomorrow," he replied, "you will hear him."

23 So the next day Agrippa and Bernice came with great pomp and entered the audience hall together with the military and civil leaders. Then Festus gave orders to bring Paul.

24 Festus said,

>King Agrippa, and all those who are present with us, you see this man about whom the whole Jewish people petitioned me both at Jerusalem and here, shouting that he ought not to live any longer.

25   I found that he had done nothing deserving death, but when he appealed to the emperor, I decided to send him.

26   But I have nothing certain to write to my lord about him. That is why I have brought him before you, and especially before you, King Agrippa, so that when there has been an examination I may have something to write.

27   It seems to me unreasonable to send a prisoner and not to state the charges against him.

---

the Jews a bone. Agrippa expressed interest in seeing Paul, so Festus promised that the very next day he would arrange for him to do so (v. 22). With pomp and circumstance, petty King Agrippa and his retinue arrived the next day. Paul was brought forth. Festus once more outlined the situation for the group that had assembled, this time telling Agrippa that he had little to write to Caesar upon sending Paul to Rome, and expressing hope that he would be able to help him in the matter after examining him. After all, Festus said, "**It seems to me unreasonable to send a prisoner and not to state the charges against him.**" He was right, of course. But he was wrong in not having released Paul when he could find no evidence for the charges made by the Jews. The fact that it seemed ludicrous to him to send Paul without a statement of the particulars, makes that all too evident. His dilemma was of his own making (as are many such foolish impasses).

CHAPTER 26

1 Then Agrippa said to Paul, "You are permitted to speak on your own behalf." So Paul stretched out his hand and made his defense:

    2   I consider myself fortunate, King Agrippa, that I am about to make my defense before you today about all those things of which I am being accused by the Jews,

    3   because you are especially well acquainted with all of the Jewish customs and issues. So then, I urge you to listen to me patiently.

    4   My manner of life, from my youth, from the beginning spent in my own nation and in Jerusalem, is known by all the Jews.

    5   They have known before about me, from way back—if they are willing to testify to it—that according to the strictest sect of our religion I have lived as a Pharisee.

    6   Now I am standing trial for putting my hope in what God promised our fathers;

    7   a promise that our twelve tribes, earnestly worshiping night and day, hope to see fulfilled. It is this hope for which I have been accused by the Jews, O King!

    8   Why should any of you think that it is incredible for God to raise the dead?

    9   I myself was convinced that I ought to do many things in opposition to the name of Jesus the Nazarene,

---

Paul's final address is recorded in this chapter. It is a magnificent defense in which Paul not only sets forth the facts of his conversion and all that led up to the moment, but also angles for Agrippa's soul. The story has been told twice before in the book of Acts, each time with the addition of a few new facts. Because Agrippa knew about most of what had happened in Palestine, and because he was acquainted with Jewish law and custom, Paul was particularly fortunate, as he said, to be able to speak before him (vv. 2, 3). He outlined his career up to his conversion, stressing the vehemence with which he persecuted the faith (vv. 4-11). Then he related in detail the events surrounding his conversion on the Damascus road (vv. 12-18). Finally he spoke about the reason for his imprisonment centering on the gospel message (vv. 19-23).

Festus interrupted him as he spoke, saying, **"Paul you're mad! Your great learning is driving you crazy!"** Paul countered this remark by telling him and the king that he was sure that **none of these things has been hidden from him,** since **this wasn't done in a corner.** There is nothing

10   which, in fact, I did in Jerusalem. I locked up many of the saints in prison by authority from the chief priests, and when they were put to death, I cast my vote against them.

11   I often punished them and compelled them to blaspheme throughout all the synagogs, and in boundless rage against them I persecuted them even to foreign cities.

12   For this reason I was traveling to Damascus with discretionary authority from the chief priests,

13   when, at noon, I saw along the road a light from the sky, that was brighter than the sun, shining around me and those who traveled with me.

14   When we had fallen to the ground, I heard a voice saying to me in the Hebrew dialect, "Saul, Saul, why are you persecuting Me? It is hard for you to kick against goads."

15   I said, "Who are You, Lord?" And the Lord said, "I am Jesus Whom you are persecuting.

16   But get up and stand on your feet. I have appeared to you to appoint you as a minister and as a witness to the facts about Me that you have seen and in which I will appear to you,

17   delivering you from your people and from the Gentiles, to whom I will send you

18   to open their eyes so that they may turn from darkness to light, and from Satan's authority to God, to receive forgiveness of sins and a lot among those who have been sanctified by faith in Me."

19   Wherefore, King Agrippa, I wasn't disobedient to the heavenly vision,

20   but first to those in Damascus, then at Jerusalem and throughout all the country of Judea, and to the Gentiles, I announced the need to repent, to turn to God and to do practices appropriate to repentance.

21   Because of this the Jews grabbed me in the temple and tried to kill me.

22   So then, I have had God's help to this day, when I stand here testifying to both small and great, saying nothing other than those things that the prophets and Moses said were going to happen—

23   that Christ would suffer, and that as the first to rise from the dead He was going to announce light both to His people and to the Gentiles.

24 As he was making this defense, Festus said with a loud voice, "Paul, you're mad! Your great learning is driving you crazy!"

25 But Paul said,

        I am not crazy, most excellent Festus. Rather, I am speaking revelatory words that are both true and sane.

26   The king understands these things, and in fact I can speak boldly
      to him, because I am convinced that none of these things has been
      hidden from him. This wasn't done in a corner!
27   King Agrippa, you believe the prophets, don't you? I know that
      you believe.
28 Agrippa said to Paul, "In a short time you are going to persuade me to
become a Christian!"

---

esoteric or mysterious about the Christian faith. Unlike the mystery religions and gnosticism of the day, it is an historical religion that could point to events about which witnesses were prepared to bear testimony. The resurrection was not hidden. The disciples talked to the Lord for forty days afterwards, at one point Jesus was seen by over 500 brothers at once, and individual women and apostles spoke with Him (cf. I Corinthians 15). Lastly, He had revealed Himself to Paul, who also then had become a witness. Paul turned to Agrippa, using this opportunity to appeal to his **belief** in the Old Testament **prophets**. If he trusted in the message of the prophets, why, then, shouldn't he believe that their message about the Messiah had been fulfilled?

Agrippa, mildly sarcastic, probably more as a put off than anything else since Paul was zeroing in on him, said, **"In a short time you are going to persuade me to become a Christian!"** Paul responded to this remark with a statement of good will in which he expressed his sincere desire that however long or short a time it took, he wished Agrippa and all who heard would become Christians (vv. 24-29).

The consensus at the conclusion of the hearing was that Paul had done nothing deserving death or even imprisonment. Indeed, as Agrippa said, he could have been set free if he hadn't appealed to Caesar. But the circumstances had led to the appeal. The appeal was going to lead to the trip to Rome. And the trip to Rome would lead to Paul's opportunity to present the gospel to the emperor of the world. All was going forward in God's providence according to the program outlined by Jesus in Acts 1:8. Nothing merely happened—then or now. Things happen in ways that further the purposes of God—whether we can discern immediately how this is so or not. Providentially, Paul would travel to Rome at the expense of the government!

This climactic speech in Acts was given before the thirty-three year old Agrippa who, for ten years, had been king of a little country East of the Jordan river called Trachonitus. Here Paul's language and style were noticeably different from what we see in previous speeches. He adapted to

29   And Paul said, "Whether short or long, I would pray to God that not only you but all who are listening to me today might become exactly as I am—except for these chains."

30   Then the king, the governor, Bernice and those who were with them got up,

31   and when they had left they spoke to one another, saying, "This man hasn't done anything deserving death or imprisonment."

32   Agrippa said to Festus, "This man could have been set free if he hadn't appealed to Caesar."

---

the occasion as he spoke to a king, a princess, a Roman governor, military officers of the highest rank, and leading men of the city. It was a great opportunity. Paul's speech is the most polished one of all. The Holy Spirit inspired it, adapting it to the occasion (cf. chapter two). When the source of Paul's message was questioned (v. 24), Paul made it clear that he was speaking **revelatory words** (v. 25; *apophtheggomai* was used here for the third time; cf. Acts 2:4, 14 for the two other occasions and for commentary on this term). Throughout the speech Paul seemed to be fishing for Agrippa. He dismissed the charges in a sentence or two, then dealt with Christian doctrine and gave his personal testimony to its truth. When he was interrupted, he turned that interruption to his advantage, making it the occasion for addressing Agrippa. Christians may learn much from the way in which the Spirit led Paul to use opportunities to witness. That is one of the major contributions of the book of Acts to the practice of counseling.

CHAPTER 27

1   When it was decided that we should sail for Italy, they handed over Paul and some other prisoners to a centurion named Julius, who was from the Augustan Cohort.
2   We boarded a ship from Adramyttium that was about to sail to ports along the coast of Asia, and set sail. Aristarchus, a Macedonian from Thessalonica, was with us.
3   The next day we landed at Sidon, and Julius treated Paul kindly and allowed him to go to his friends to receive care.
4   From there we put to sea and sailed under the lee of Cyprus, because the winds were contrary.

The long chapter that comes next shows how difficult travel was in those days, and how Paul shone forth as the leader of the trip, even as a prisoner. Once more, we see that God was in charge, bringing Paul to his next ministry in Rome. Paul's witness was exemplary, in whatever circumstance he found himself. By referring to this account, a counselor is able to show fearful counselees how God can provide for their needs, save them from danger, and give them opportunities for evangelism; they learn how they may endure hardship while, at the same time, turning every difficulty into an asset for Christ.

The first eight verses tell of the various ports of call where they stopped and of the course that they followed. Paul, acting as a prophet, warned them not to travel on the next leg of the journey; because of the wintry weather, ships avoided the waters across which they had to go (vv. 9, 10). But the centurion, as would seem the sensible thing to do, listened to the captain of the ship rather than to Paul. So, ignoring Paul's counsel, they set sail (vv. 11, 12). Sounds like many counselees I have known. They follow what seems to be the right way; but if it is contrary to God's word, it is always the wrong one (cf. Proverbs 14:12).

At first all looked good; but before long they encountered a **hurricane** and were driven off course by it. After many days of desperate measures, they abandoned all hope (vv. 13-20). But at that point Paul came through. First, he reminded them that he had told them they would have problems (v. 21). But then he advised them about the future. They were to have another opportunity to listen to the Lord. He had received a visit from an **angel** who assured him there would be no loss of life, but only of the ship. He made it clear that the reason they would be safe was because

162

5   After sailing across the sea that is off Cilicia and Pamphylia, we came to Myra in Lycia.

6   There the centurion found an Alexandrian ship sailing to Italy and got us on board.

7 For a number of days we sailed slowly, and with difficulty arrived off Cnidus. But because the wind didn't allow us to go on, we sailed under the lee of Crete off Salmone.

8   We sailed along with difficulty, and came to a place called Fair Havens, near which was the city of Lasea.

9 When much time had been lost, and the voyage was now dangerous, since the autumn fast had already gone by, Paul advised them, saying,

10   "Men, I see that the voyage will be accompanied by injury and much loss, not only of the cargo but also of our lives."

11   But the centurion was persuaded by the captain and owner of the ship rather than by the things that Paul said.

12   Since the harbor wasn't suitable for wintering, the majority decided to set sail from there, hoping that they might be able to arrive at Phoenix, a Cretan harbor that looked to the southwest and the northwest, and winter there.

13 So when a south wind blew gently, they thought they had what they wanted, so they raised anchor and sailed along close to the shore of Crete.

14   Before long a hurricane, called the northeaster, swept down,

15   and when the ship was caught by it and unable to hold its own against the wind, we gave way and were driven by it.

16 Running under the lee of a small island called Clauda, with difficulty we managed to secure the lifeboat.

17   After hoisting it aboard, they undergirded the ship with ropes. Because they were afraid that they might run aground on the Syrtis sandbars, they lowered the sea anchor and were driven along that way.

18   But as we were so violently battered by the storm, the next day they began to jettison the cargo.

19   And on the third day, with their own hands they threw the ship's tackle overboard.

20   When neither sun nor stars appeared for many days, and the storm kept pressing us hard, all hope that we might be saved was now abandoned.

21 Since they had gone without food for so long, Paul then stood up in their midst and said,

> Men, you should have listened to me and shouldn't have set sail from Crete, and avoided this injury and loss.

22   But now I advise you to take heart, because there will be no loss of life among you, but only of the ship.

23   I say this because this very night there stood by me an angel from the God to Whom I belong and Whom I also serve, saying,

24   "Don't be afraid, Paul; you must stand before Caesar. And God has given you all those who are sailing with you."

25   So cheer up, men; I believe God that it will be exactly as I have been told.

26   But we will have to run aground on some island.

27 Now when the fourteenth night came, as we were being driven along in the Adriatic Sea, about midnight the sailors suspected that they were approaching land.

28 When they sounded, they discovered they were in twenty-fathom-deep water. A bit farther on they sounded again and found it was fifteen fathoms.

29 Fearing that we might run aground somewhere against rocks, they let down four anchors from the stern and prayed for the day to come.

30 The sailors were trying to escape from the ship and had lowered the lifeboat into the sea under the pretense of letting down anchors from the bow,

31 so Paul said to the centurion and to the soldiers, "Unless they stay in the ship, you cannot be saved."

32 Then the soldiers cut the ropes of the lifeboat and let it fall away.

33 As the day was about to dawn, Paul encouraged them to eat some food, saying,

       Today is the fourteenth day that you have been expectantly waiting and have gone without food.

34   I urge you to eat some food; you'll need it to come through alive, since not a hair of anybody's head is to perish.

God had determined that Paul would **stand before Caesar** (vv. 22-26). The blessings of association with a believer (even in such ways as the passengers on this ship received them) are apparent from Paul's words in verse 24. For the sake of His own, God often is very gracious to others as well. This principle holds true in many other ways as well.

When they appeared to be running aground, the sailors determined to abandon ship. But Paul warned the centurion, "**Unless they stay in the ship, you cannot be saved.**" This time he listened to Paul (vv. 27-32). He cut the ropes to the lifeboat, making escape impossible. Finally, Paul encouraged them to **eat** something since they would need it when making the effort to reach shore (vv. 33, 34).[1] He took some bread, thanked God in front of them, and they all ate (vv. 35, 36). At daybreak they saw a **bay** with a **beach** close where the ship ran aground on a **sandbar**. The stern broke into pieces. The soldiers wanted to kill the prisoners, but because

---

[1] He always kept his faith up front even in desperate circumstances.

35   When he said this, he took some bread, gave thanks to God before all of them, broke it and began to eat.

36   So they all took heart and ate some food themselves.

37   (In all, we were two hundred seventy-six persons on board.)

38   When they had eaten enough food to satisfy them, they lightened the ship, throwing out the wheat into the sea.

39   Now when day came, they didn't recognize the land, but they saw a bay with a beach on which they wanted to bring the ship aground if they could.

40   So they threw away the anchors into the sea, loosened the ropes tied to the rudders, hoisted the foresail to the wind and headed for the beach.

41   But the ship ran aground on a sandbar where two bays met; the prow held fast, but the stern was broken up by the waves.

42   Now the soldiers' plan was to kill the prisoners lest any should swim away and escape,

43   but the centurion, wanting to save Paul, prevented them from carrying out this intention. He ordered those who could swim to jump overboard first and head for land,

44   and the rest to float in, some on planks, others on other things from the ship. And in this way everybody safely reached land.

---

the centurion wanted to save Paul, he wouldn't let them. They jumped overboard, floated on boards or whatever they could find that would hold them up in the water, and by various means all 276 persons finally managed to reach land—just as Paul had predicted.

Here, once again, we see the providence of God at work. Everything appeared to be against the outcome. At every point it seemed as if Paul would fail to make it to Rome. But God is sovereign. Whether he had to swim, float to land or get there some other way, God would have Paul reach Rome. Until he had finished his course, nothing could stop him. That also is true of every Christian. Whatever purposes God has for him *will* be accomplished and, as has often been said, he is indestructible until then. Counselees often fail to remember this fact and need frequent reminders of it.

CHAPTER 28

1 After we had arrived safely, we discovered that the island was called Malta.

2 The inhabitants were unusually kind to us. They started a fire and welcomed us all, because it had begun to rain and was cold.

3 When Paul collected a bundle of sticks and put them on the fire, a viper, driven out by the heat, fastened itself to his hand.

4 When the inhabitants saw the creature hanging from his hand, they said, "Certainly this man must be a murderer; even though he has escaped the sea, justice hasn't allowed him to live."

5 However, he shook off the creature into the fire and suffered no harm.

6 They expected him to swell up or suddenly fall down dead. But after waiting a long time and seeing nothing amiss had happened to him, they changed their minds and called him a god.

7 Now in the vicinity were lands that belonged to the chief official on the island, whose name was Publius. He received us and entertained us hospitably for three days.

8 It so happened that Publius' father lay sick with fever and dysentery. Paul went in to him, prayed, put his hands on him and healed him.

The passengers from the ship discovered that the island on which they landed was **Malta**. Those who lived there were unusually **kind** to the weather-beaten, drenched men who reached land. They started a **fire** by which they could dry and thaw out. Paul helped, it is interesting to note. While doing so, a snake bit him and fastened itself to his hand. The inhabitants immediately thought that this meant he was a **murderer**. But when he shook it off and nothing happened to him they changed their minds and called him a **god** (vv. 1-6). The fickleness of superstitious pagans is almost unbelievable. Moreover, the quickness with which they made these judgments is remarkable. But some Christians act similarly. The minute something bad happens to someone, they think it is an act of **justice** working against him. The minute that it turns out well, they change their minds. The fact is that in God's providence circumstances do not come with interpretations. Each individual puts his own interpretation on them—very frequently the wrong one. Christians must be careful not to act like pagans (or even like Job's counselors) in this regard.[1]

Publius, the chief official on the island, entertained the men for three

---

[1] For a fuller discussion of this matter see my book *The Christian's Guide to Guidance.*

9   When this took place, the rest of the people on the island who were sick came too and were given medical treatment.

10   They greatly honored us, and when we sailed they supplied all that we needed.

11   After three months we sailed on an Alexandrian ship with the Twin Brothers as its figurehead, that had wintered in the island.

12   We docked at Syracuse and stayed there for three days.

13   From there we made a circuit and arrived at Rhegium. After one day a south wind blew up, and on the second day we came to Puteoli.

14   There we found some brothers, who invited us to stay with them for seven   days.

And that is how we went to Rome.

15   Now the brothers from there, when they heard about us, came as far as the Appian Forum and the Three Taverns to welcome and escort us back. When Paul saw them, he thanked God and took courage.

16   When we entered Rome, Paul was allowed to stay by himself with the soldier who guarded him.

---

days. His father lay sick and Paul prayed, placed hands on him, and healed him (vv. 7, 8). Then people from all over the island who were sick came (as the word Luke, a physician, uses indicates) for **medical treatment**[1] (v. 9). Probably some healing, at least, was not miraculous in nature. The inhabitants honored them and supplied them with all they needed when they were ready to set sail once more (vv. 9, 10). Finally, they reached Italy at the port of **Puteoli** where Paul and his companions were able to fellowship with some brothers (vv. 11-14). Then they went to Rome. The brothers from Rome, hearing in one way or another about Paul's coming, went out to **meet** him and **escort** him back into the city. Nowhere else do we read of an honor such as the one they accorded Paul. It also gave Paul new courage to continue his tasks there (v. 15). How fitting for believers to go out of their way to honor and greet those who have been so useful in the kingdom. There is so little of that attitude in the church today; everyone, it seems, wants to pick out flaws in leaders or treat them simply as "one of the gang." There was a different spirit of respectful gratitude manifested here that would be well to cultivate in our day. Counselors have opportunities to encourage this in counselees.

Paul was given a great deal of freedom when he reached Rome (v. 16). As soon as he was settled, he sent for the Jewish leaders in Rome

---

[1] Perhaps Luke was involved in helping as well.

17 After three days he called together to him the Jewish leaders, and when they had gathered, he said to them,

> Brothers, although I have done nothing against my people or the customs of our fathers, I was handed over as a prisoner into the hands of Romans,

18   who, when they had examined me, wanted to free me, because there was no ground for putting me to death.

19   But when the Jews protested, I was forced to appeal to Caesar, although I didn't have any charge to bring against my nation.

20   For this reason I have asked to see you and speak to you, since it is because of Israel's hope that I am bound with this chain.

21 They said to him,

> We haven't received any letters from Judea about you, nor has any of the brothers coming here reported or said anything bad about you.

22   But we think that it is right to hear from you yourself what your views are, since we know that people everywhere are talking about this sect.

23 When they had arranged for a day to meet with him, they came to his lodging in large numbers. And he explained the matter to them, testifying about God's empire and trying to persuade them about Jesus from the Law and the Prophets, from morning till evening.

24   Some were convinced by what he said; others disbelieved.

---

since he could not go to meet them at the synagogs. He explained exactly what had happened and the reason he was there under guard; and he made it clear once more that it all had to do with **Israel's hope** (of the Messiah; v. 20). They had heard nothing about Paul and the trouble that he encountered at Jerusalem and wanted to hear from Paul's own lips what he had to say. They had heard a lot about Christianity, but they needed more information (v. 22). This attitude was a reasonable, open one.

So they arranged for a day to meet and came to the place where he was staying; he explained everything to them, persuading them from the Scriptures about Jesus being the Christ (v. 23). Some believed, others did not (v. 24). Since they couldn't agree, they left after Paul had spoken a final word (which could be the final word in many counseling situations). He quoted Isaiah where the **Holy Spirit** through Isaiah said they would have closed eyes, ears and hearts. He then made it clear that God was bringing into the church Gentiles who would believe if the Jews wouldn't. It was the typical order: to the Jews *first*. . . then also to the Gentiles. For two full years, awaiting his trial before Nero, Paul remained in his own

25 Since they were in disagreement with one another, they left after Paul had spoken one parting word:

> The Holy Spirit was right when He said to your fathers through the prophet Isaiah,

26 **Go to this people and say,**
You will hear and hear, but you won't ever understand
you will look and look, but you won't ever see.

27 **This people's heart has grown thick,**
and their ears have become hard of hearing,
and they have closed their eyes
lest they might see with their eyes,
or hear with their ears,
or understand with their heart
and turn, and I shall heal them.

28 Let it be known to you, then, that this salvation from God has been sent to the Gentiles— and they will listen.

29 [1]

30 Now he stayed there for two full years in his own rented quarters and welcomed everybody who came to see him.

31 He preached God's empire and taught about the Lord Jesus Christ with great boldness and without hindrance.

---

[1] Some MSS add vs. 29: *After he said this, the Jews left, arguing vigorously among themselves.*

---

rented quarters welcoming all who came to visit and preaching to numbers of people. He was not hindered. And notice, the summary of what he taught was **God's empire**, the very same message that John the Baptist and Jesus had preached. John announced that it was soon coming, Jesus said that it was now time for it to appear, and Paul announced that it had in fact appeared. Note also, though Paul was a prisoner, he taught **boldly**. When one knows that he is doing as God wishes, that he is teaching the truth, he has no reason not to be bold in proclaiming it. How can there be biblical boldness among eclectic counselors? There is no assurance of truth; there is no authority to minister.

The book of Acts holds many values for the biblical counselor. The boldness of proclamation, mentioned here, the providence of God at work in the course of human events, the insistence on doing what God says even when it means disobeying authorities (operating outside of their God-given sphere), the willingness to adapt, the ability to suffer patiently and many more, are elements from which counselors and their counselees may profit greatly. Obviously, there is more in Acts than could be considered in this volume. Go back again and again to Acts to see the Lord Jesus at work through His Spirit. See how Luke glorifies Him, not those who serve Him. Notice how God's plans never skip a beat. Don't miss the importance of chapter 20 for the counselor.

Acts is a book about the sovereign acts of God. Because of that there is much that encourages, much that guides, much that challenges. Use it for all of these purposes. Acts is unique in the Bible. It shows the progress of the church as it spread from Jerusalem to Rome. It raises difficulties, shows how they were met, and indicates the ways and means of meeting problems today. Acts focuses on using the political system, knowing and insisting on one's rights when appropriate, and showing a willingness to forego those rights when it is not essential to assert them. It demonstrates the authority of the church and the importance of becoming a part of it; it gives no ground to those who stand aloof from it. Acts is a multifaceted book that reaches out in all sorts of directions. Every counselor needs to be familiar with it. He dare not neglect it, or his counseling will be weakened by that neglect.

With this volume, I complete my commentary on the New Testament. I recognize that in many ways it is inadequate, but hope nevertheless that it will do much good. There is a great deal that is suggestive in these volumes. You must take it and run with it yourself, applying principles and practices to various concrete situations that you encounter as counselors. It is not filled with stories or citations or experiences. It is a commentary series that relies on the exegesis of verses so as to point from that exegesis to the implications for biblical counseling. It assumes that the reader has a basic commitment—however firm—to the fundamental principle that the Scriptures "alone" are sufficient for life and godliness. May your counselees discover the reality of this truth as you counsel them confidently, boldly, pointedly, helpfully and effectively from the Word of the living, gracious, and sovereign God.

www.ingramcontent.com/pod-product-compliance
Lightning Source LLC
LaVergne TN
LVHW051236080426
835513LV00016B/1612